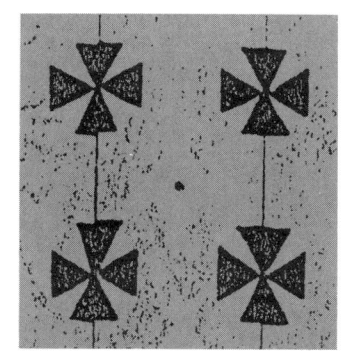

Classic
NEW MEXICAN FURNITURE

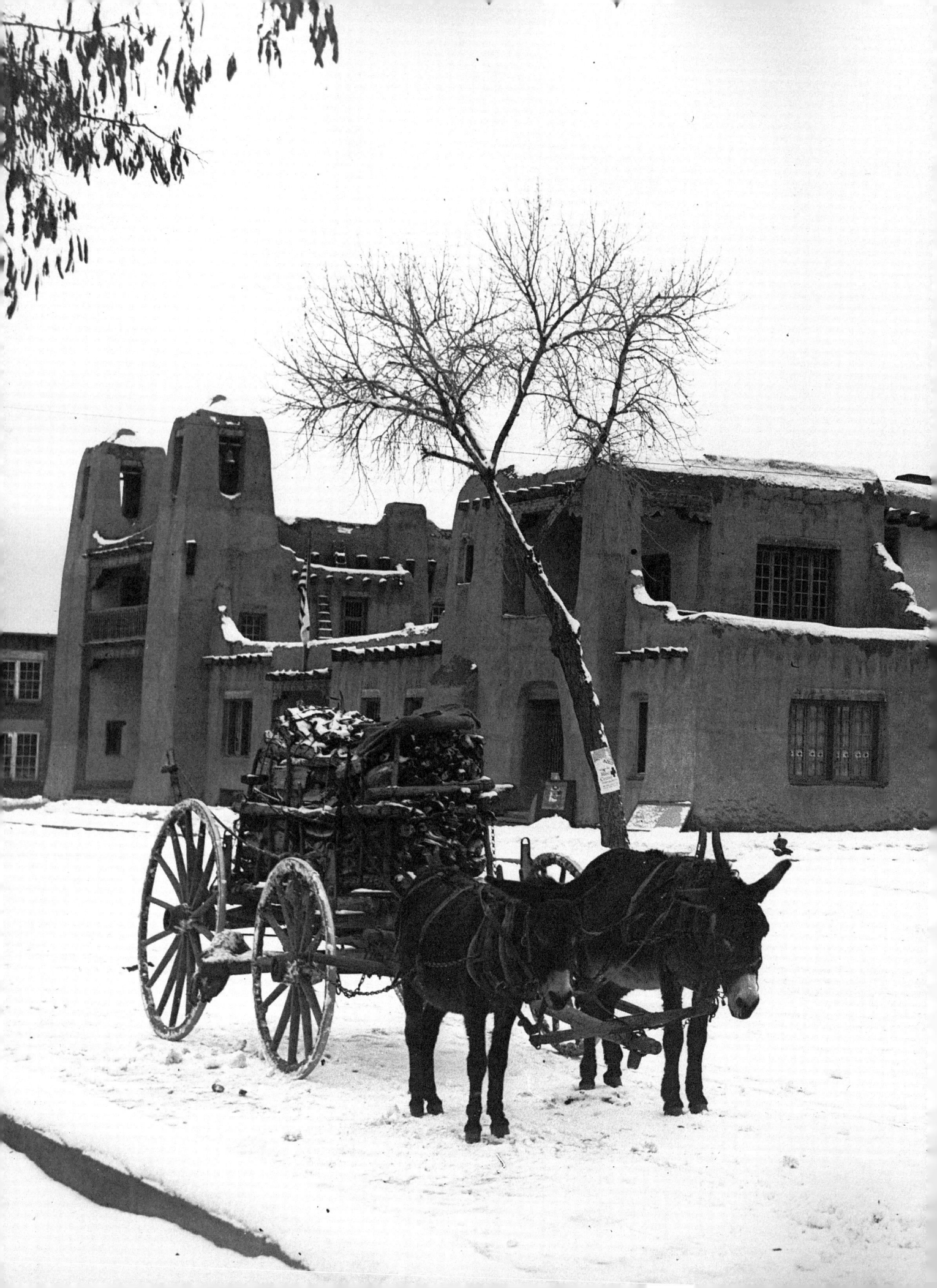

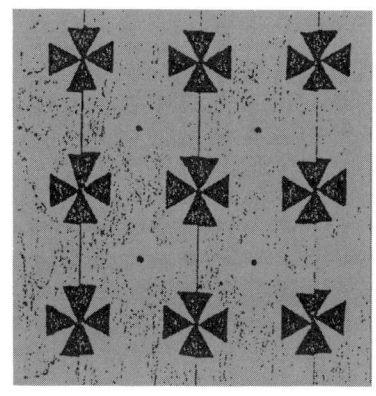

Classic
NEW MEXICAN FURNITURE

A HANDBOOK OF
PLANS AND
BUILDING TECHNIQUES

KINGSLEY H. HAMMETT

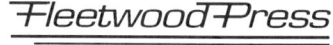

Fleetwood Press

SANTA FE, 1996

This book is dedicated to my wife Jerilou with whom anything is possible.

First Edition
Printed in the United States of America
10 9 8 7 6 5 4 3 2

Book Design by Molly McCord, M&M Design

Cover photo is a trastero built in 1935 in Roswell, New Mexico, by Domingo Tejada.
Courtesy of the Roswell Museum and Art Center.

Historic photographs:

Page 4: Wood cart on the Santa Fe Plaza in winter, December, 1918. Photo by Wesley Bradfield. *(Museum of New Mexico, Neg. No. 12986)*

Page 10: The Mexican Band, Monticello, New Mexico, ca. 1900. Photo by Henry A. Schmidt. *(Museum of New Mexico, Neg. No. 58627)*

Page 14: Fiesta, Santa Fe, New Mexico. *(Museum of New Mexico, Neg. No. 11707)*

Page 28: Fine Arts Museum, Santa Fe, New Mexico, 1917. *(Museum of New Mexico, Neg. No. 2889)*

Page 95: Crossing the stream at Chimayo. Photo by Burt Harwood. *(Harwood Foundation Museum, #A3)*

Library of Congress Catalog Card Number: 95-83905
Hammett, Kingsley H.
    Classic New Mexican Furniture: A Handbook of Plans and Building Techniques. —1st ed.
    Includes bibliographical references and index.
    ISBN 0-9648256-0-0

Also by the author:

Crafting New Mexican Furniture: A Handbook to Design, Plans, and Techniques
Red Crane Books, 1994

FLEETWOOD PRESS
2405 Maclovia Lane
Santa Fe, New Mexico 87505
(505) 471-4549

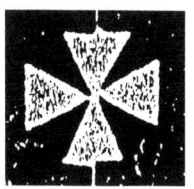

I want to thank the following individuals whose gracious contributions made this book possible: the staff of the Museum of International Folk Art, particularly Robin Gavin, curator of the furniture collection, who willingly gave her time and knowledge, and Eleanor Voutselas, curator of the Museum of International Folk Art photo archives, who secured most of the photographs in this book; Donna Pierce, curator of the Spanish Colonial Arts Society;

Acknowledgments

Christy Skinner, associate collections manager of the School of American Research; Teresa Hays Ebie, registrar of the Roswell Museum and Art Center; Lonn Taylor and Dessa Bokides, whose monumental work *New Mexican Furniture: 1600 -1940* has inspired so many New Mexican woodworkers; Mary Peck, whose photographs from *New Mexican Furniture: 1600 -1940* appear here; David Hart, who took the photographs in the chapter on design techniques as well as of two of the pieces; Laz Cardenas, a very talented woodworker from Taos, New Mexico, whose hands and handiwork appear in the techniques section; John Schmelz and Shelley Brock for their drawings; Bill Felong; Carol Caruthers and Beth Snyder.

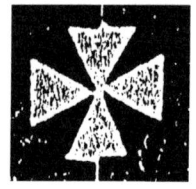

Contents

✠

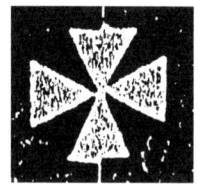

✠

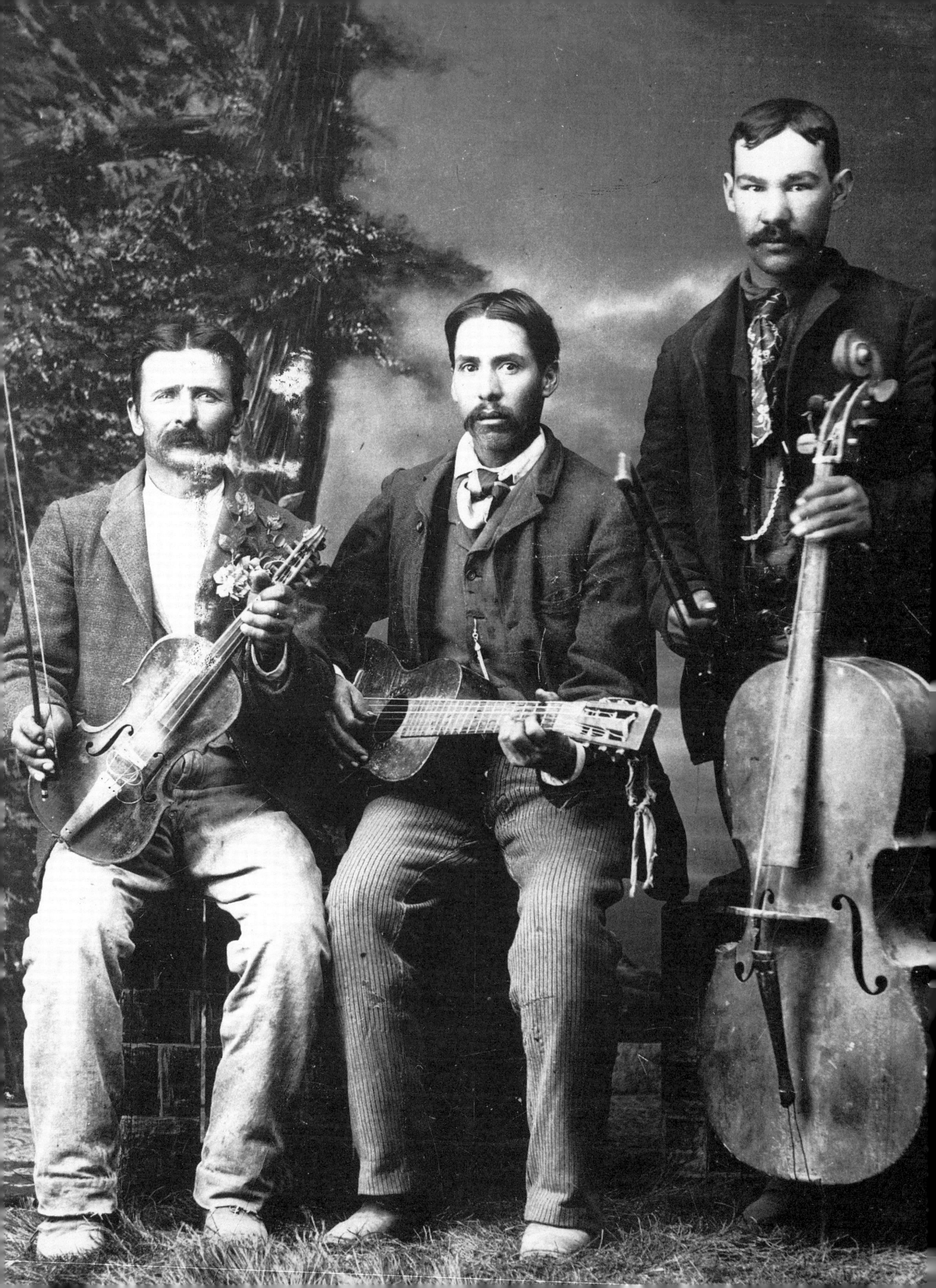

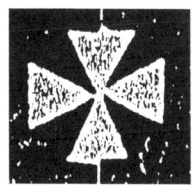

ORIGIN OF NEW MEXICAN STYLE

The romance of the New Mexican or "Santa Fe style," hyped around the world in recent years in everything from faux adobe homes to howling pink coyotes, is most authentically captured in the unique furniture of the area. This style has been 400 years in the making, and its evolution — from the earliest Spanish conquistadors, to the struggling Hispanic settlers, to the conquering Yankees, to the invasion of artists, tourists, and Anglo-American archeologists, architects, and historians — tracks with the history of this harsh and turbulent land. Out of this complex history has grown a unique style and tradition, ever changing to meet the needs and tastes of the moment, that continues to be practiced throughout the state.

Introduction

SPANISH COLONIAL PERIOD: 1598-1821

Reaching Santa Fe from Mother Spain was an arduous task in the sixteenth and seventeenth centuries, and what little furniture existed in those early years was hauled up the Camino Real to serve the needs of the Catholic Church. When those pieces were rebuilt and reworked until nearly nothing original was left, it fell to the Spanish colonialists to craft their replacements.

The wood of choice was the ponderosa pine which was felled, split, and adzed to a workable thickness and fashioned into large pieces of furniture, no two of which were alike. Each was held together with through mortise-and-tenon joints with square pegs and wedges to keep things tight.

"Carpinteros" visually relieved the massive boards of some of their weight by carving Spanish and Moorish motifs in relief — pomegranates, rosettes, shells, lions, and scallops. Additional embellishments included heavy grooving and cutouts along table aprons and bottom rails and hand-carved spindles and splats inspired by the window grilles then popular in Spain.

Trasteros, or cupboards, had doors that swung on pintle hinges. Crests, cut into the shape of fans or scallops, often adorned the top front and sides of such pieces and were held there in dados cut in the legs which extended above the top of the cabinets. Deep carvings suggesting corn stalks, rain, and the heavens on some surviving pieces indicate they may have been built on Indian pueblos.

ANGLO-AMERICAN PERIOD: 1821-1900

The opening of the Santa Fe Trail in 1821 brought Anglo settlers along with sawn planks, the frame saw, molding planes, and the Empire style so popular back East. To meet the demands of the new taste, European-born craftsmen began to build furniture forms that had not yet entered the Hispanic vocabulary — chests of drawers, bookcases, washstands, and writing desks.

By 1880, the demand for home furnishings was met by the newly arrived railroad that could ship into the territory goods mass produced on the East Coast. But that didn't stop craftsmen at work in the isolated villages of northern New Mexico from taking these new influences and developing their own charming, vernacular style that saw many traditional pieces decorated with intricate cutouts, turnings, and applied wood panels reminiscent of the Empire, Greek Revival, Mission, and Craftsman styles popular at that time.

Bed and chair legs took on a decided Empire curve while their backs were made from more finely turned and tapered spindles. Trasteros became wardrobes under the Anglo-American influence and were topped with crown moldings. Some were highly painted and "grained," while others sported punched tin fronts like their Hoosier cabinet cousins from the Midwest.

SPANISH COLONIAL REVIVAL PERIOD: 1920 - PRESENT

New Mexican furniture making lapsed into idleness during the first twenty years of this century as the needs of locals were met by factory-produced imports. But interest in traditional New Mexican style snapped awake with the new state's entry of a Pueblo-style building in the California-Panama Exposition in San Diego in 1915. Two years later, the ideas from the San Diego exposition — the soft, rounded curves of adobe, levels that stepped up in seemingly random patterns, and roof beams of peeled pine logs that protruded through the exterior walls — found their way into the Museum of Fine Arts built on the southwest corner of the Santa Fe plaza. The new "Santa Fe style" was born.

This style was a mixture of Spanish colonial and Pueblo Indian elements. The designs carved into the massive beams and corbels in the new museum were adapted from drawings made at historic sites up and down the Rio Grande. Similar themes, including chip carving painted in dull reds and blues and protruding tenons adapted from the Mission and Craftsman styles, were included in the furniture built for the museum's Women's Board Room and became signatures of the Spanish Revival period through the 1930s and on into today.

IMAGINATIVE FINISHES

Most New Mexican furniture built today is finished with a simple stain, a clear finish, and maybe a coat of wax. But evidence has shown that that might not always have been the finish of choice in colonial New Mexico. Recent research using high-powered microscopes has revealed that many pieces of colonial furniture, some dating back several hundred years, were in fact brightly painted. It's been speculated that when the territory became part of the greater United States and factory-made furniture was imported via the railroad, traditional pieces were rejected for the new and were put out in the barn or on the back patio to suffer the ravages of time. When they were discovered in the early twentieth century, they had lost their colorful hues and had turned weathered brown, leading copiers to believe it was always so.

Some of the pieces offered here, like the collection in the Women's Board Room, were and are still highly colored in blues and reds. One favorite chest (see p. 46) has panels in red and green. Feel free to use your imagination, for it appears that in colonial New Mexico any finish was deemed acceptable.

THE IMPORTANCE OF PROPORTIONS

I offer this book with the simple hope that anyone interested in building a piece of "southwestern" furniture will turn first to the authentic source of all such designs: the style that evolved in New Mexico over the last 400 years.

Shoppers today can find "southwestern" furniture from North Carolina to California with generous contributions available from Texas, Colorado, and Arizona. But all such pieces are mere copies or an interpretation of the style that originated in New Mexico when the conquistadors first made their way north up the Rio Grande river from the interior of Mexico.

In recent years such interpretations have taken alarming turns for the worse, and mainstream woodworking magazines have published stories on how to build atrocious looking, bogus "southwestern" pieces with plywood and oak using routers with precise patterns, with only passing reference to the specific details that give New Mexican furniture its unique style.

Taking such liberties with New Mexican style reminds me of the children's game called "Telephone," where a secret whispered in one ear bears no resemblance to the message that comes out far down the line. In similar fashion, many of these ersatz "southwestern" interpretations of New Mexican-style furniture serve only to further dilute the beauty and simplicity of the original pieces and shift their lovely proportions all out of balance.

The pieces selected for this book are but a sampling of all that has been collected and preserved by the Museum of New Mexico and the Spanish Colonial Arts Society, Inc., and what exists in other public and private collections. They appear classified by type — chests, tables, benches, etc. — and are presented roughly in chronological order. If there are more chests than tables, that's probably because history has left us more chests to collect.

They are here simply because these are the pieces I want to build myself. In subsequent books I expect to offer additional drawings of pieces, both from the classic periods as well as from the Spanish Colonial Revival period of the early- to mid-twentieth century.

I don't believe that anyone should become a slave to any particular detail or dimension offered in this book. This collection is not intended to serve as a guide to creating perfect museum reproductions. Of course, those who want to invest the time to create such copies are welcome to do so. But for the average furniture maker in search of a beautiful piece, this book offers many opportunities to create something of lasting beauty that may suggest, but not completely copy, the original.

My hope is that furniture built from this book is done so with respect for the original. If the plan calls for material that is 1 inch thick, don't use 2x4s. Use 4/4 material. The beauty of these pieces is in their proportions, and the key to creating a piece that's in keeping with its classic look is building it to the correct overall dimensions.

It is difficult to reduce a drawing of a 7-foot-long chest onto a 7-inch piece of paper, so in some cases it may be difficult to read every dimension as given. If you feel the need for a shop-size drawing you may order an 18-inch by 24-inch copy of any particular plan. Ordering details are offered in the back of the book.

Use your imagination and if you like what you build, send along a photograph. But above all, have fun!

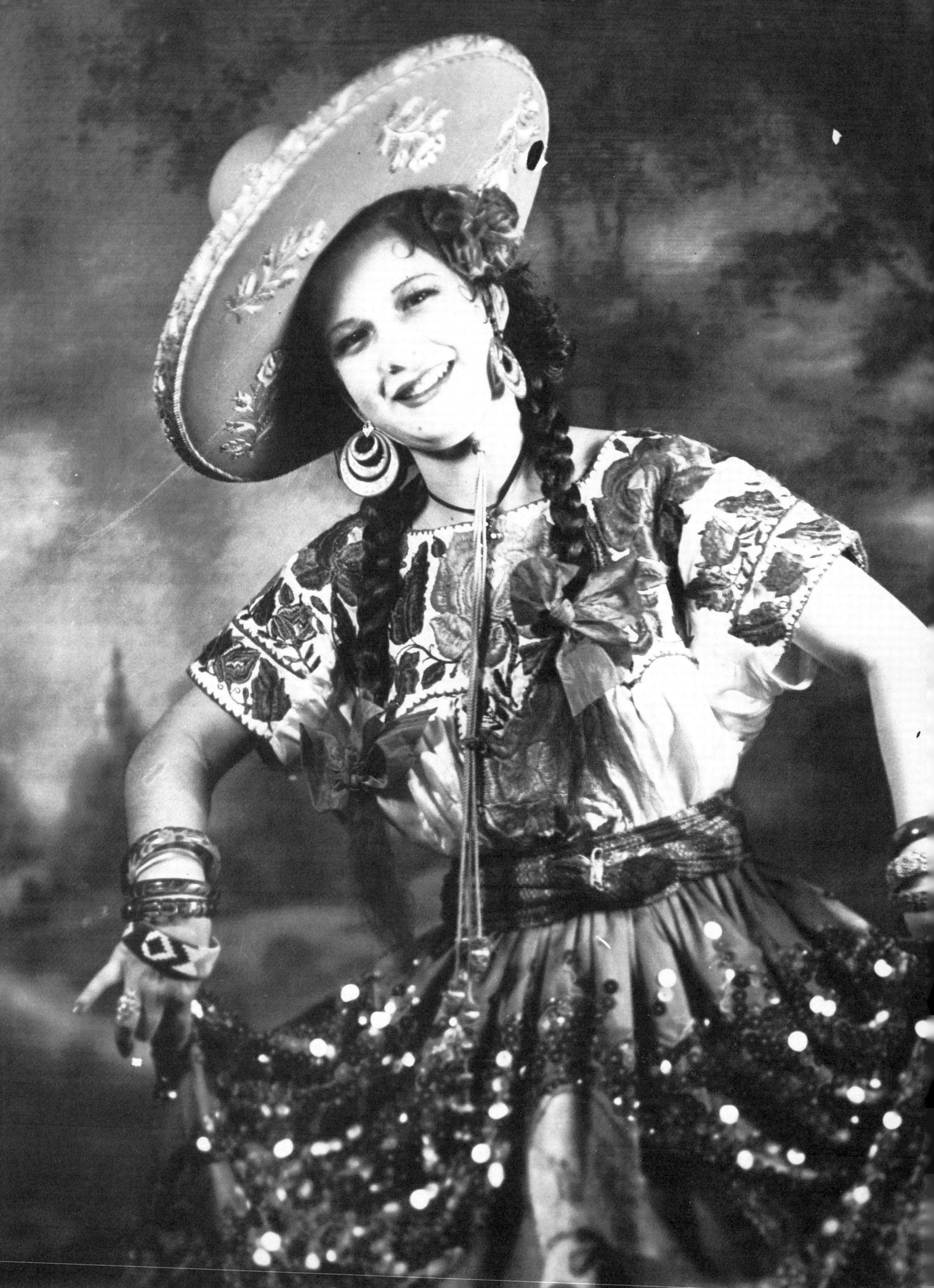

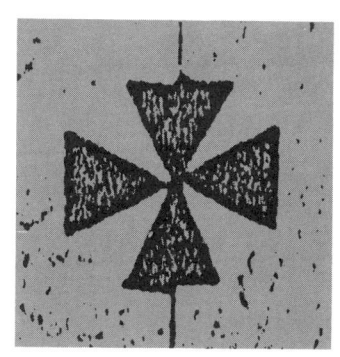

Traditional Details and
DECORATIVE EMBELLISHMENTS

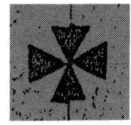

Techniques to Re-create Traditional Details and Decorative Embellishments

New Mexican furniture traditionally was made from large ponderosa boards with a few hand tools and certainly no power-driven ones. The most popular joint, and the one most often seen among the pieces offered in this book, was the overlapping through mortise-and-tenon, with a peg to achieve maximum strength and holding power.

Raised panels and geometric designs cut in relief were created with planes and chisels, not routers and plywood guides! The panels floated in dados cut the length of the piece's legs or door rails and stiles.

To relieve the blank mass of the pine planks, carpinteros developed a number of different design details that became recurring themes in New Mexican furniture. Some have their roots in the sacred symbolism of Spain and Europe. Others are drawn from the striking New Mexico landscape and Native American culture. After each detail presented, you can turn to a piece where that particular detail is employed.

I recommend that you re-create several of these design details in the same way colonial carpinteros made them — with chisels and gouges. To achieve the best results, take your time and do it the old-fashioned way. If your chisel slips and you cut out a chip of wood, don't worry. It happened to them, too, and it's what gives New Mexican furniture its charm.

Other embellishments may be created with a hand saw, back saw, saber saw, table saw, radial arm saw, or band saw. Take a little sandpaper to the resulting sharp edges to give the piece a softer, rounder look.

The names I have given to these design details are somewhat arbitrary and may not be found in everyone's lexicon. They are used simply to describe the look of the finished detail. Here is how you can create each of them:

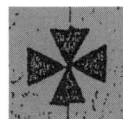

USING CHISELS AND GOUGES

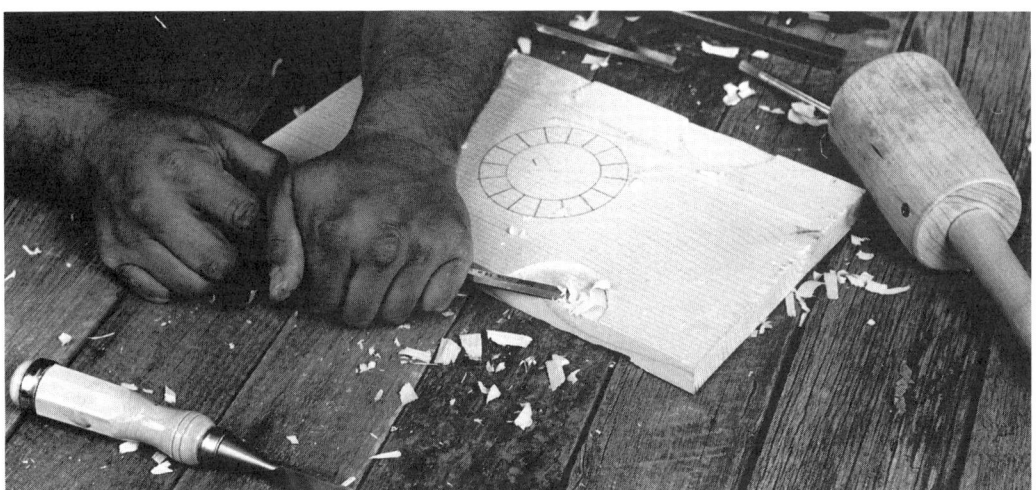

✠ GEOMETRIC RELIEF CARVING

Once you've drawn your geometric pattern on your stock, score the lines with a utility knife followed by vertical blows of the chisel. Remove the material to a depth of about 1/8 inch. Holding the chisel almost vertically, come back and clean up the edge of the cutout where the chisel blows left straight marks (see p. 30).

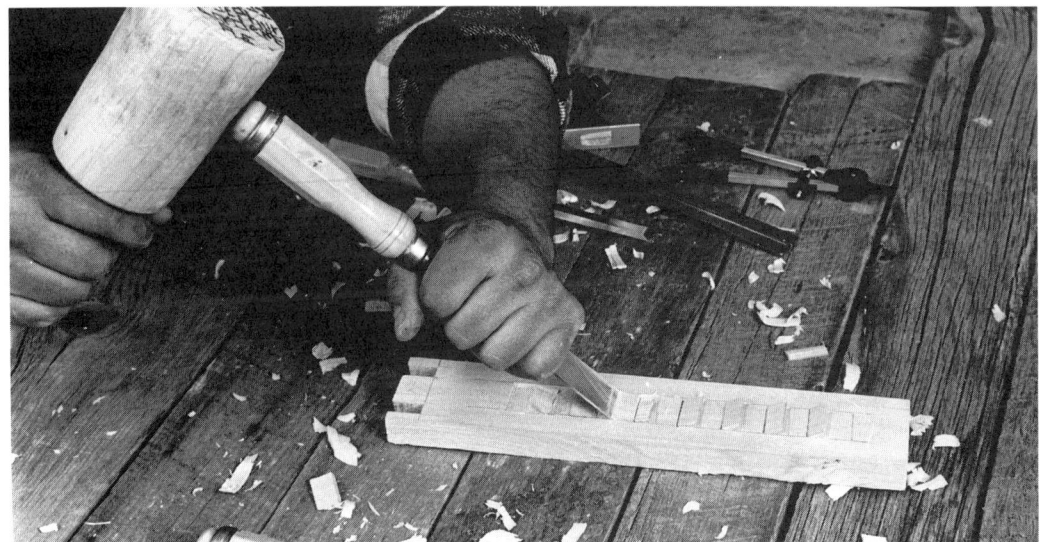

✠ BASKET WEAVE CHIP CARVING

This is actually a series of shallow "V's," one after the other. Start by laying out a 1-inch-wide band down the piece and draw a perpendicular line every inch so the entire strip is divided into 1-inch squares. Score the outside lines with a utility knife (making two passes to cut deep enough). Then whack at the perpendicular lines with a 1-inch chisel.

Beginning at the middle of each square, push forward and down with the chisel (with the bevel facing downward) and stop at the bottom of each perpendicular chisel cut. Once you have cut the full length of the piece in one direction, turn the stock end-for-end, and repeat the process so the chisel cuts meet at a shallow "V."

If they fail to meet cleanly, go back and gently work the chisel with a back-and-forth motion of the wrist down the face of the cut until they do. This time, have the bevel of the chisel facing upward. You can clean out any waste caught in the corners with the utility knife.

The end result will resemble a basket weave, particularly when one facet is painted in one color, and the opposing facet in a different, contrasting color. Red and blue is one very traditional combination (see p. 30).

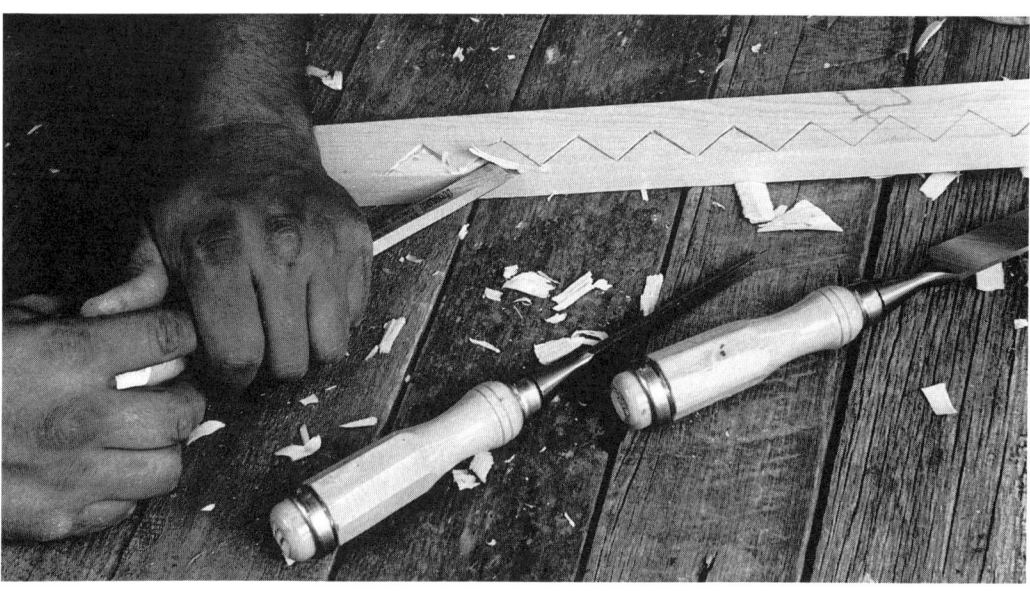

✠ SERRATED EDGE

Lay out the sawtooth pattern along one edge of your stock. With a flat chisel take a whack at each line. Go back and remove each chip to a depth of about 1/8 inch (see p. 30).

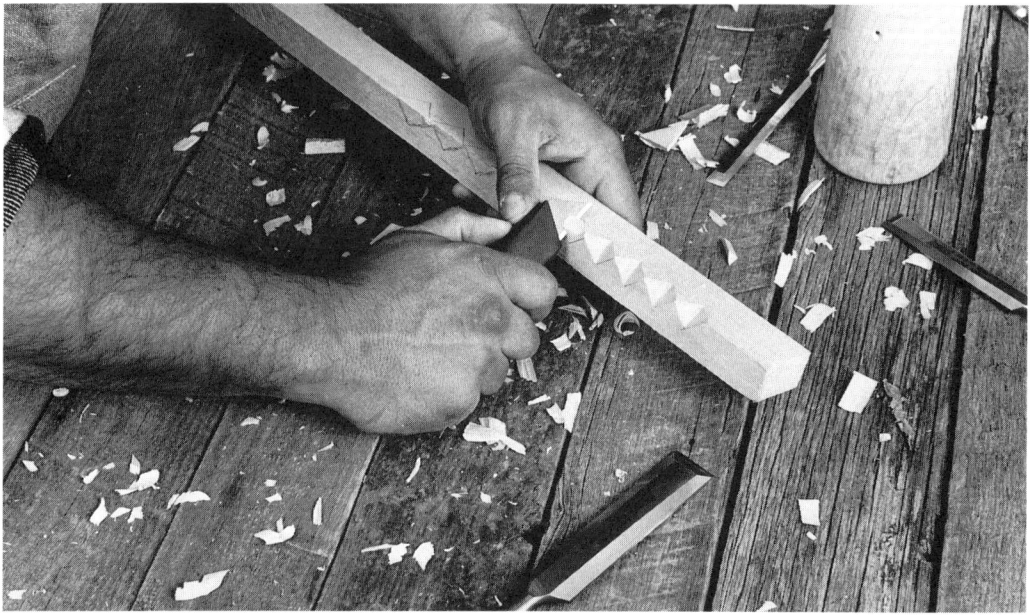

✠ SAWTOOTH CHIP CARVING

Using a sharp utility knife, simply cut and remove a series of "V"-shaped pieces along the edge of your stock (see p. 30).

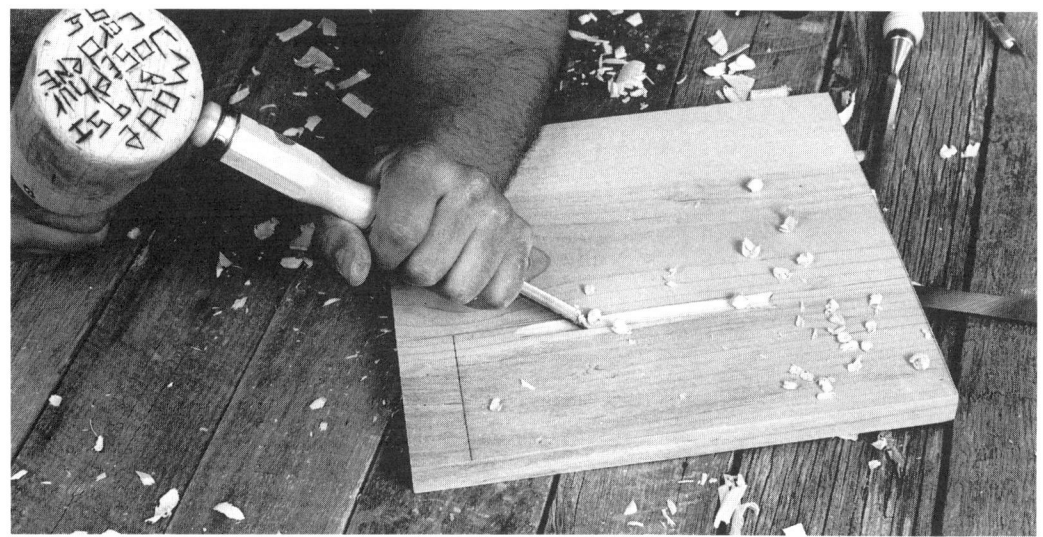

✠ GOUGE AND BEAD CARVING

Traditional craftsmen were always partial to beads and grooves, a task made easier after decorative block planes made their way into the New Mexico Territory following the opening of the Santa Fe Trail in the 1820s. Museum pieces show a great deal of use of the three-bead design (see p. 21).

To make a single bead or groove, take a fairly small radius gouge, cut down about 1/8 inch, and then tap straight and flat the length of bead you want to create. As in carving bullets (see below), some people find they have greater control when pulling the chisel toward them rather than pushing it away. Experiment and see which method you find more comfortable.

To avoid stripping out an unsightly chip, it may be better to start at the far end of a particular bead and work your way back to the starting point in several smaller segments rather than trying to carve the entire length in one pass. You might do most of the bead with a mallet and then clean it up working the gouge by hand. Again, experiment and see which works best for you (see p. 54).

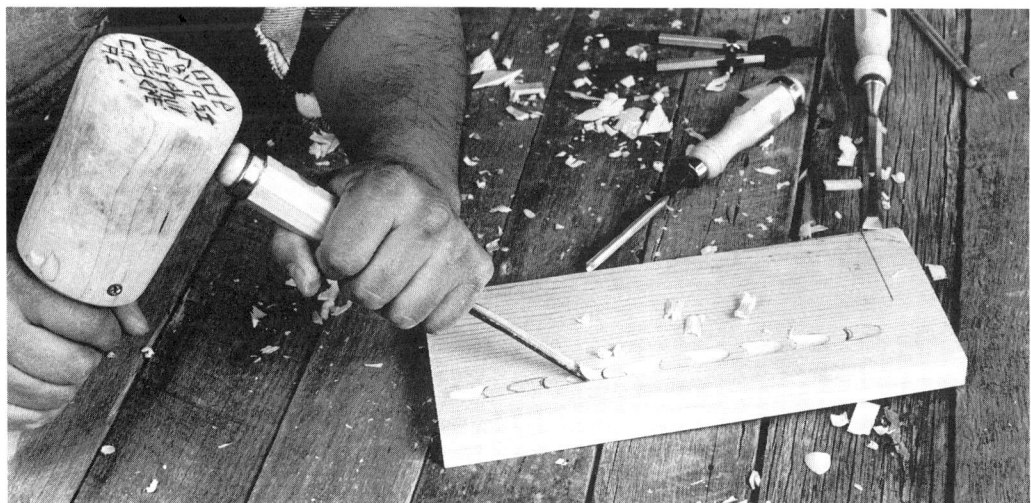

✠ BULLET CARVING

Bullets are created with gouges of varying sizes following a line you've laid out with a pencil. To make a right-facing bullet, hold the gouge with the concave surface facing to your right and cut into the stock with one vertical downward blow. Then move the gouge about an inch to the right, and come back to the left with a series of softer blows, cutting downward until you meet the first cut. When the chip is removed, the hollowed-out space will resemble the profile of a bullet (see p. 56).

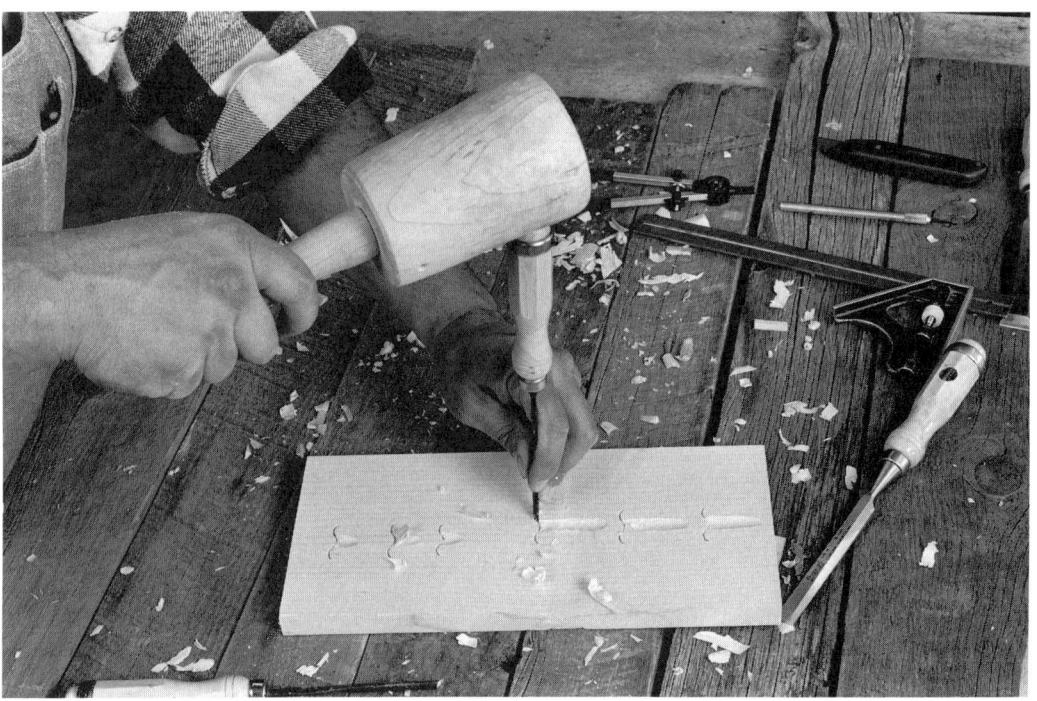

✠ RAM'S HORNS

There are two versions of the ram's horn detail. The first looks like a single bullet with two horns coming off the top, which are made by whacking the gouge down vertically.

In the second version, a series of vertical blows with the gouge are curved into a sweeping pattern. At the bottom of the curve, the gouge blows are set next to each other. At the top of the curve, the pattern switches and the direction of the gouge tip alternates to create an "S" pattern. If you are right-handed, try holding the gouge in your left hand down closer to the point, supporting the tip with your middle and ring fingers, rather than higher up on the handle. You might find you have more control (see p. 72).

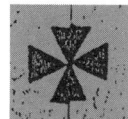

USING HAND AND POWER SAWS

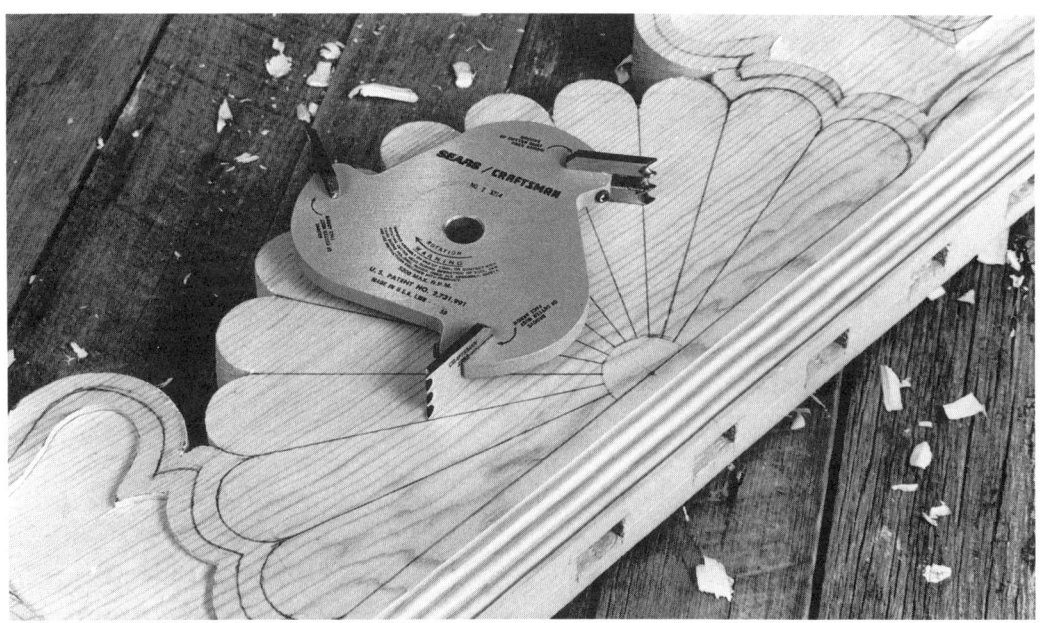

✠ **BEADS AND GROOVES**

The one-, two-, and three-bead groove was a very popular design detail. I use both single- and triple-bead cutter profile knives set in Delta molding cutter heads in my table saw. (You might also use the Sears #9-3114 molding cutter kit.) A similar effect can be achieved by cutting a kerf with the table saw blade set no more than an 1/8 inch high. Cut as many (or as few) parallel lines as you like. For a hand-carved look, you can soften the sharp edges left by the saw blade with a flat chisel (see p. 60).

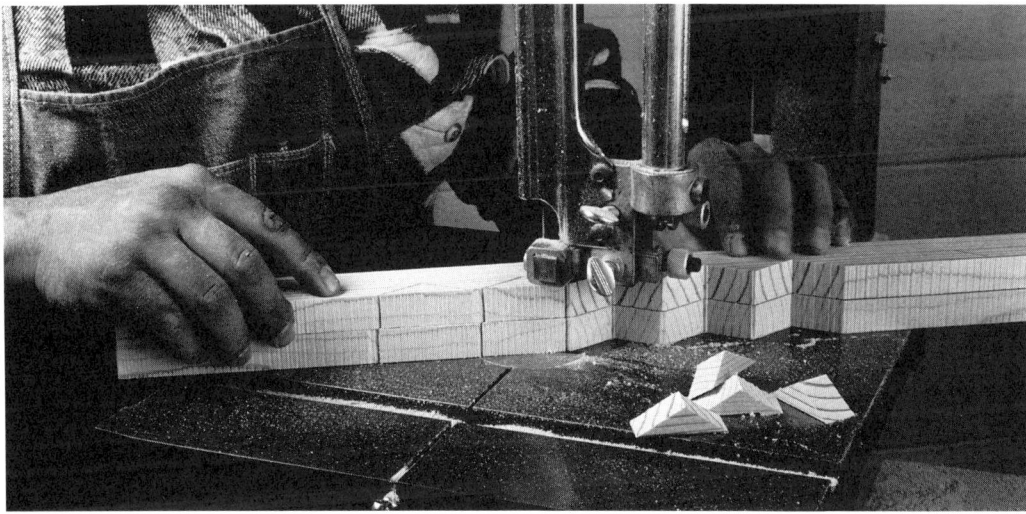

✠ **GEOMETRIC PROFILES**

Any of these profiles — the "M" (see p. 70), lightning bolt (see p. 68), bow tie (see p. 64), tulip (see p. 70), scallop (see p. 66), and step-and-mesa designs (see p. 60) — may be cut with either a power or hand saw. The preferred method is on a band saw.

To cut a scallop outline, strike a series of parallel lines the length of the piece, three or so inches apart and perpendicular to the length of the piece. Hold a jar top or other arc tangent to the vertical lines and the top of the work piece, and scribe the curves. Cut the pattern on the band saw or with a saber saw.

A very popular element adopted from the Native American culture is the "step-and-mesa" design. The geometric corners suggest the profile of a typical pueblo dwelling or apartment house as well as the outline of the surrounding mountains and mesas. This detail shows up both in chair and table aprons (see p. 50) as well as on the top of chair legs (see p. 72).

If you are creating apron or rail pieces that are not too wide, you can cut this pattern on a radial arm saw with some dado cutters. Clamp together all the pieces that will get the same design and lay out the pattern on the face, along the top, and down the right-hand side of the stack. Remove the material, beginning with the deepest cut first, then raise the saw blade in increments to do the shallower cuts. Larger pieces can be cut with a saber saw or on the band saw.

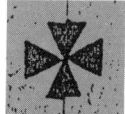

DIAGRAMS OF GEOMETRIC PROFILES

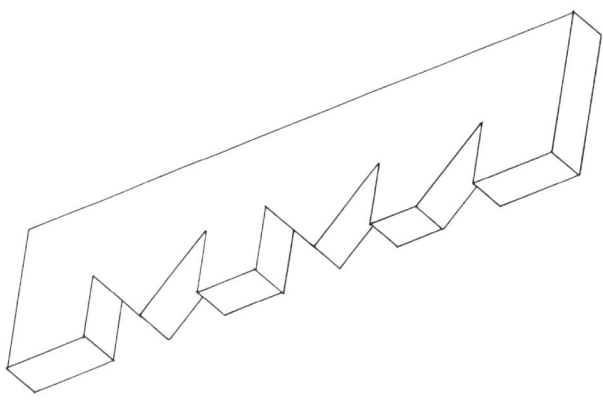

"M"

(See p. 70)

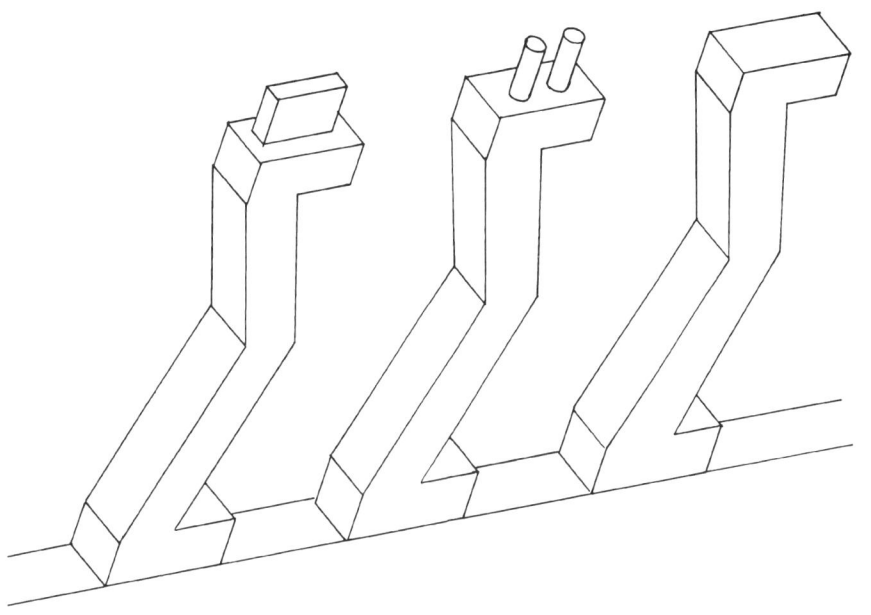

LIGHTING BOLT

(See p. 68)

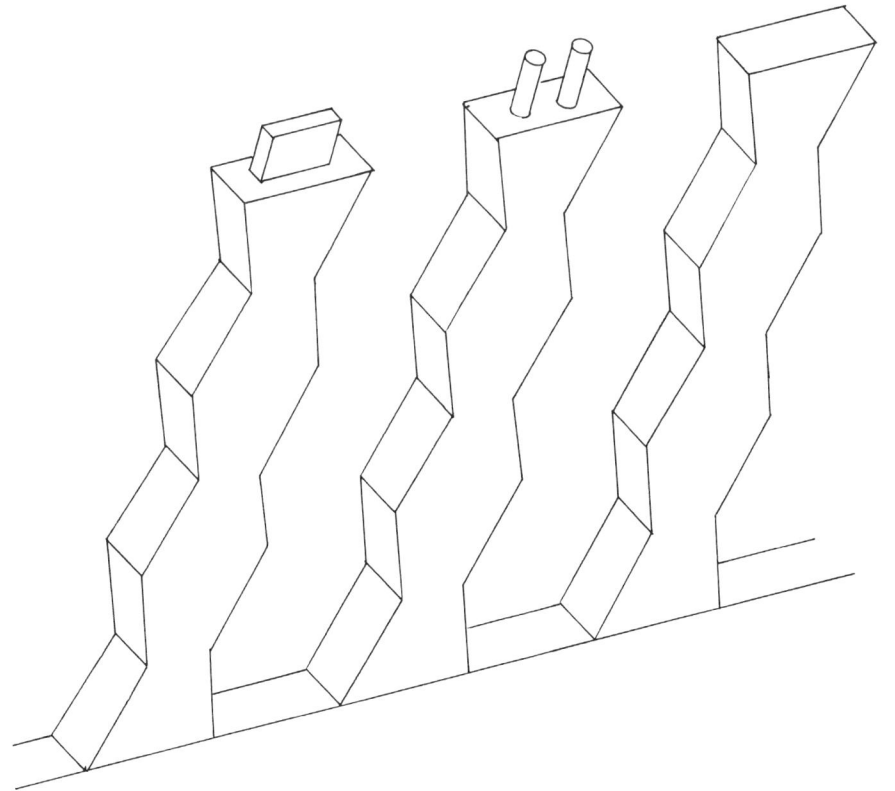

BOW TIE

(See p. 64)

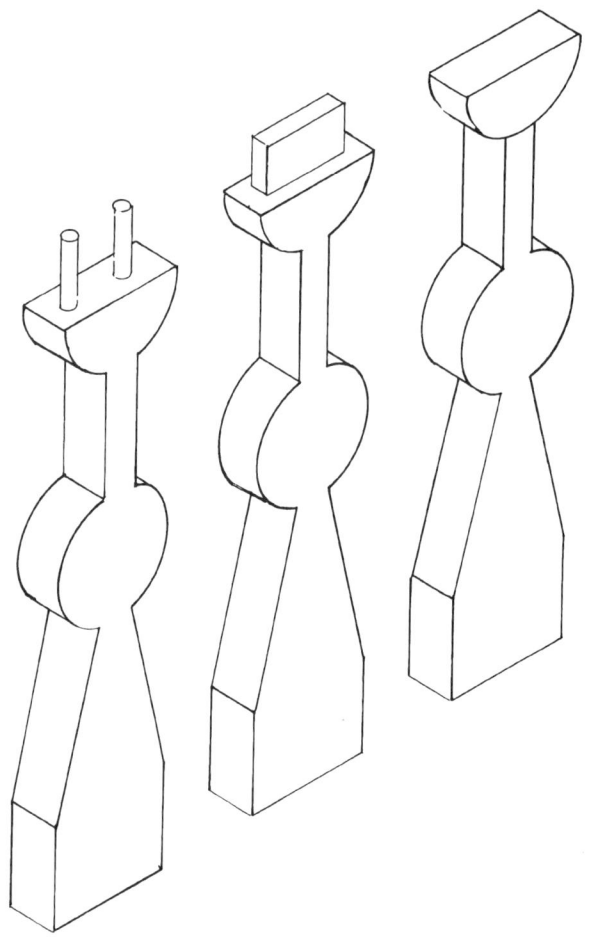

TULIP

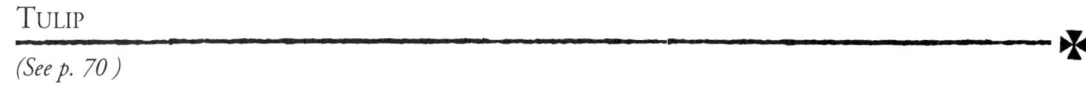

(See p. 70)

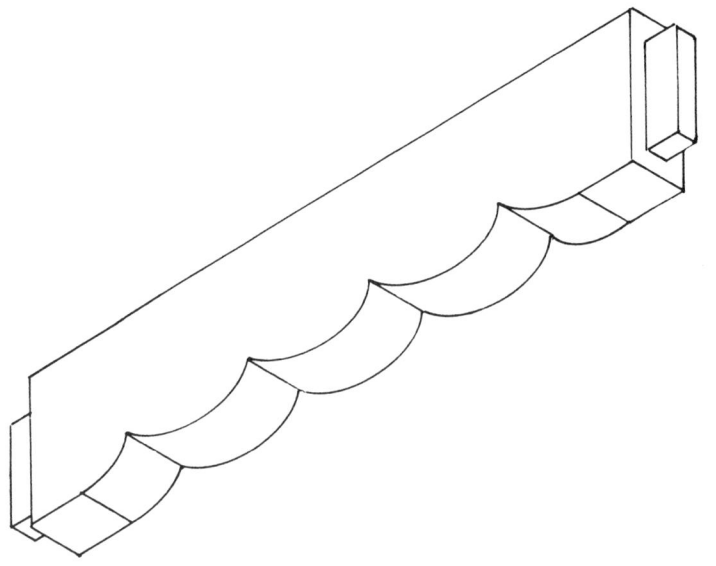

SCALLOPS

(See p. 66)

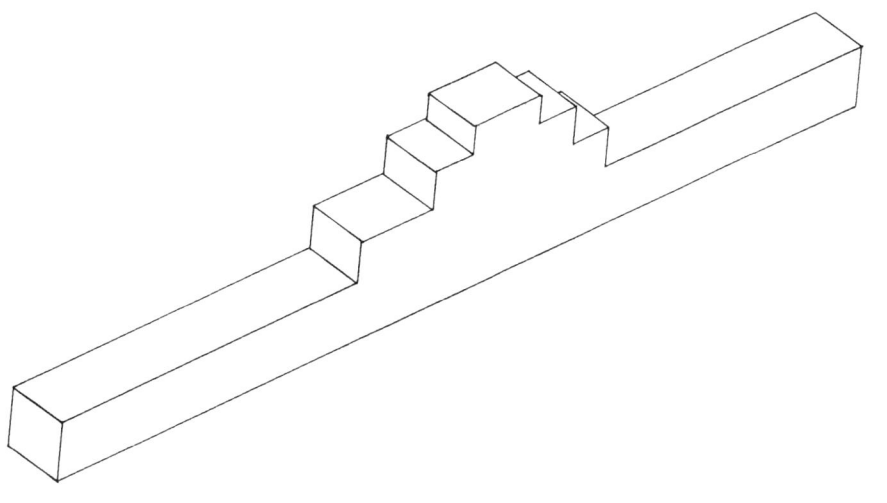

STEP AND MESA

(See p. 50)

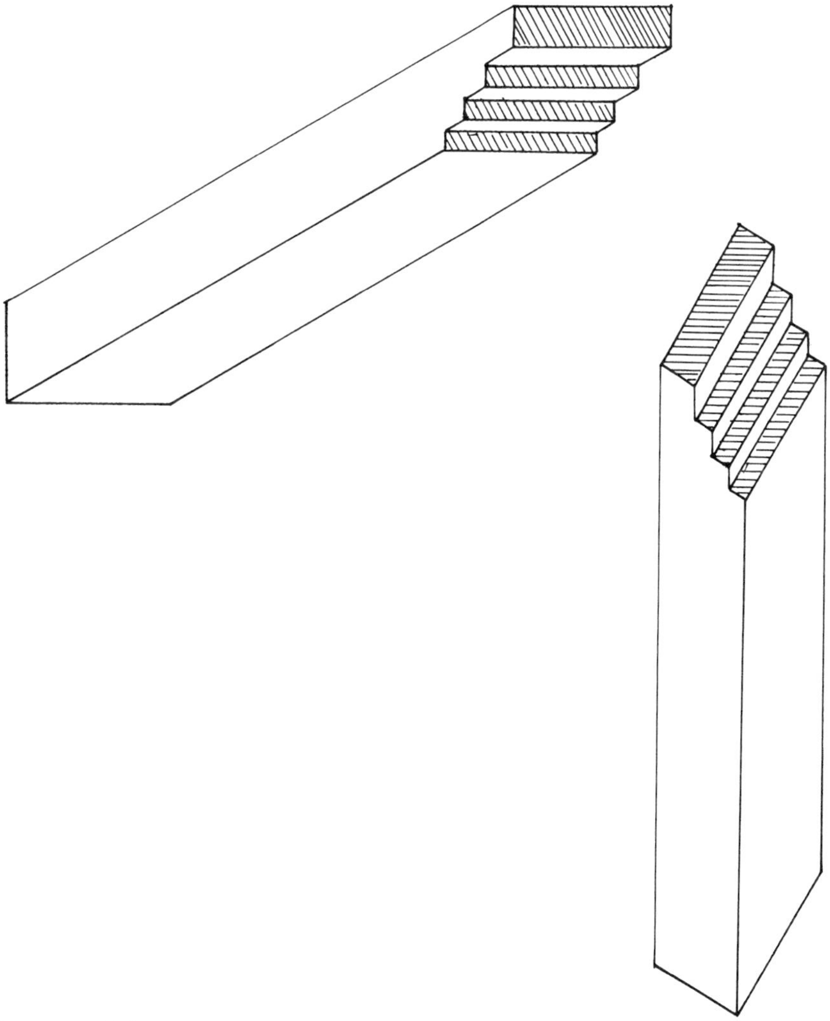

STEP AND MESA

(See p. 72)

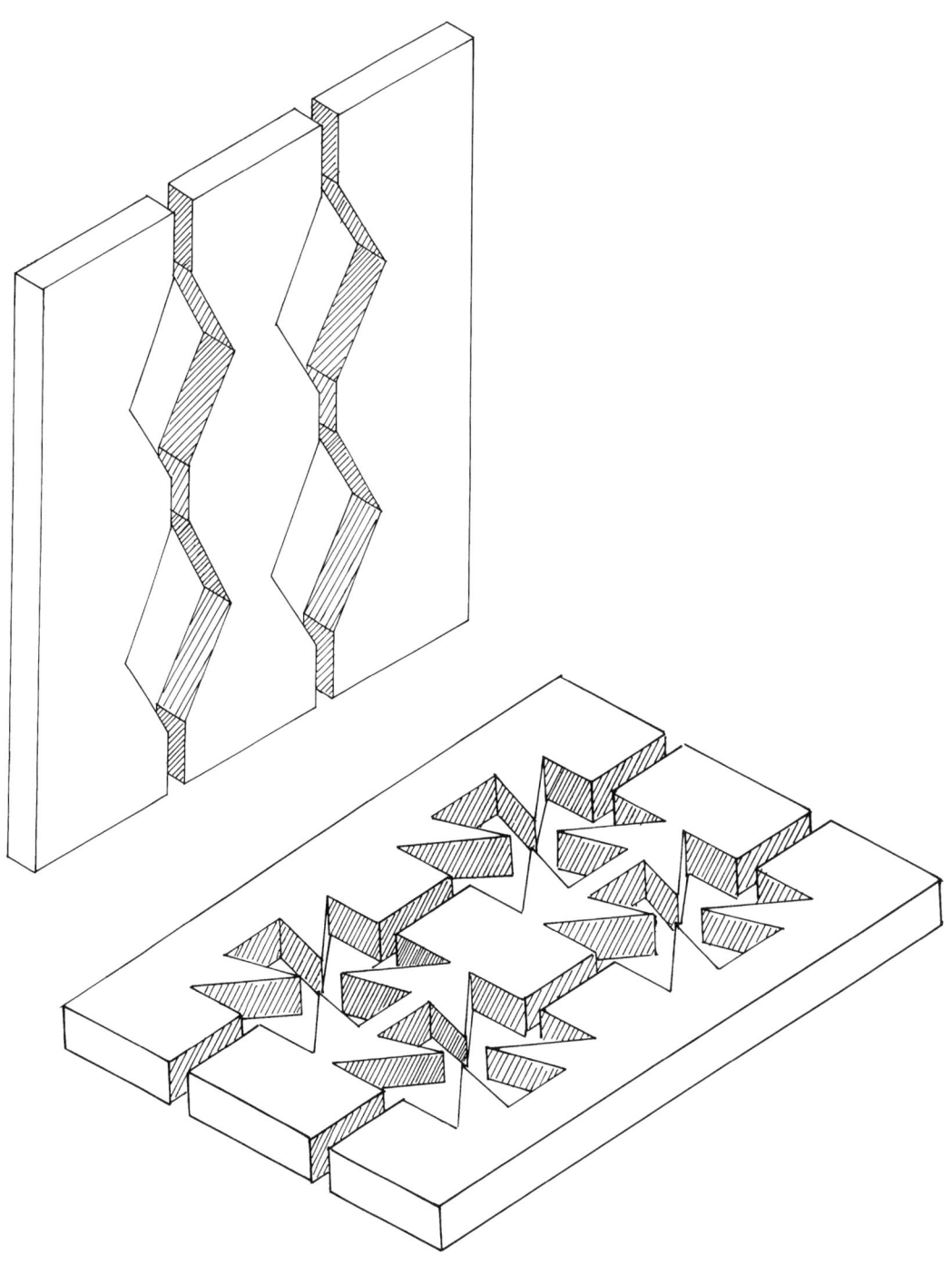

Negative Space

Beautiful effects can be achieved through the use of "negative space," or the pattern that remains after material is removed. A few of the many popular patterns include the cruciform (see p. 86), step-and-mesa (see p. 62), and diamond designs (see p. 64).

Begin by taking the piece in which the pattern will appear and ripping it in two. Hold the two halves together and cut out the pattern on the band saw as above. When you put the two halves back together, the light shining through will outline your cutout pattern.

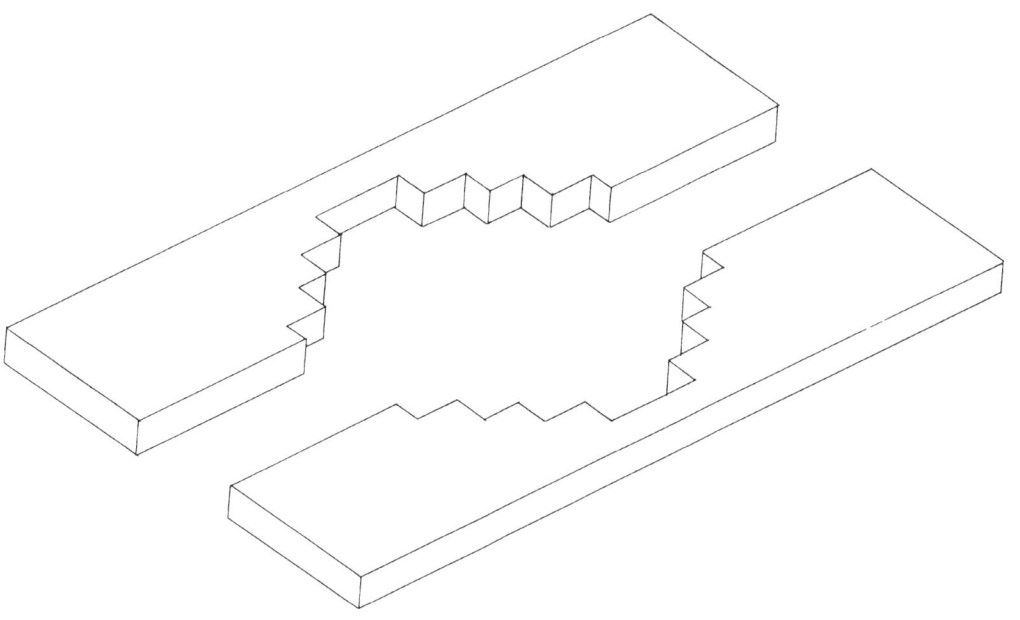

APPLIQUÉ

Chests were one of the most popular pieces of furniture on the frontier and were used to both store and transport food, clothing, and valuables. Colonial craftsmen very often would make a simple chest look more complicated by building a plain box with simple butt joints and decorating the corners and surface panels with fancy moldings and cutout designs (see p. 46). Cut your patterns on a band saw or with a saber saw and nail and glue them to the outside of the piece.

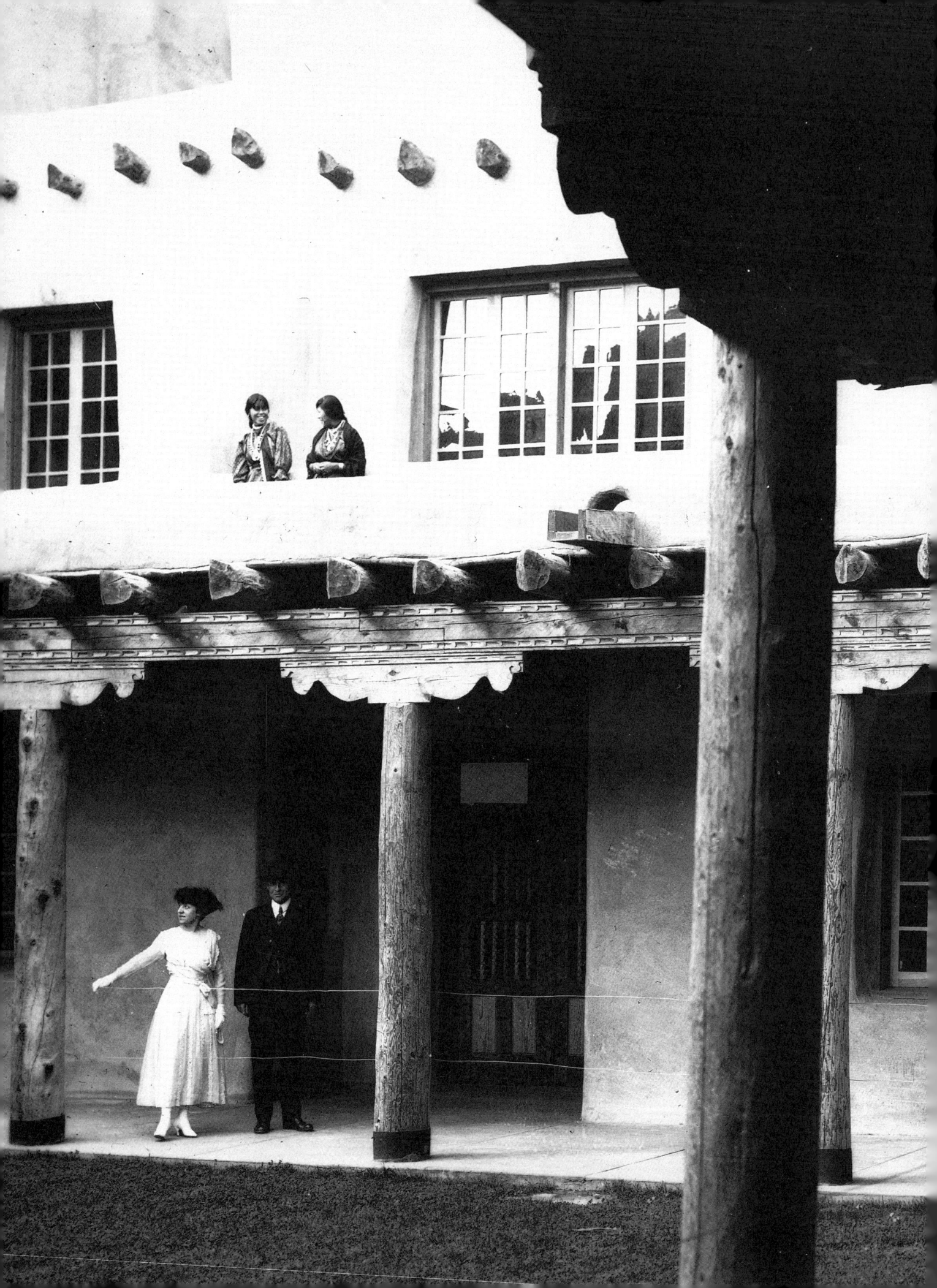

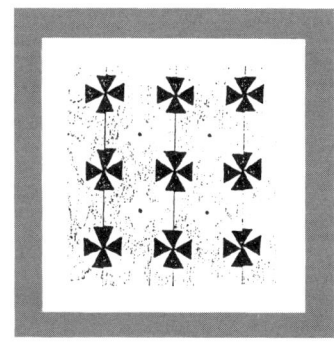

Photographs and
DIMENSIONED DRAWINGS

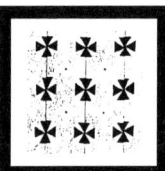

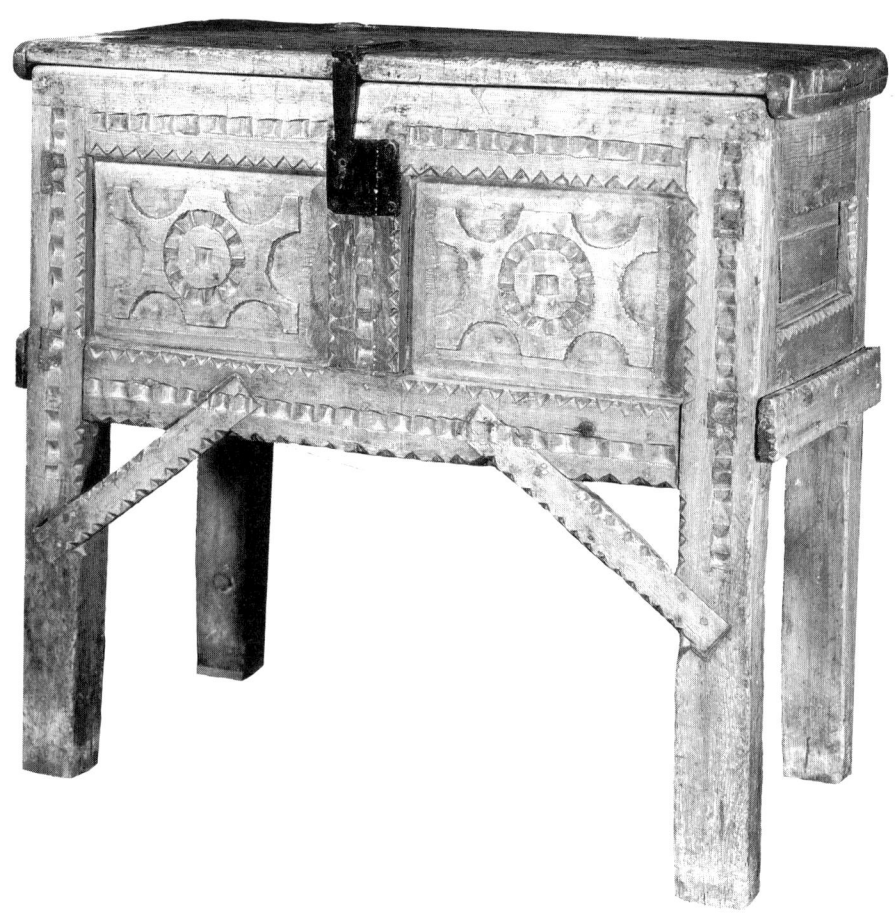

Chest on Legs with Diagonal Braces

BY THE END of the eighteenth century, chests were made with their own legs. This one, built around 1800 of adzed boards with the outer sides smoothed by planes, has diagonal braces for additional strength. Note that the diagonal braces were fastened to the bottom rail, and the tenons of the side rails fastened to the legs, before the basket weave chip carving was cut through. *Spanish Colonial Arts Society, Inc. Collection on loan to the Museum of New Mexico, Museum of International Folk Art, Santa Fe, New Mexico (FW-101).*

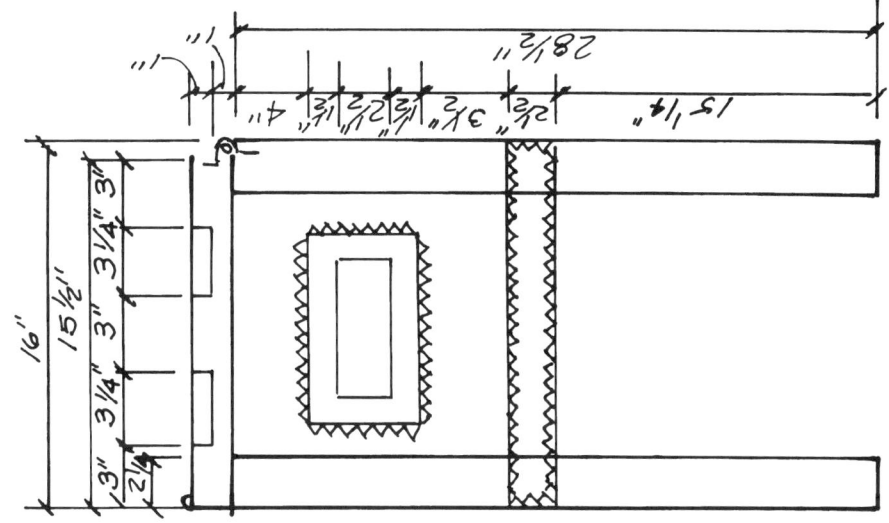

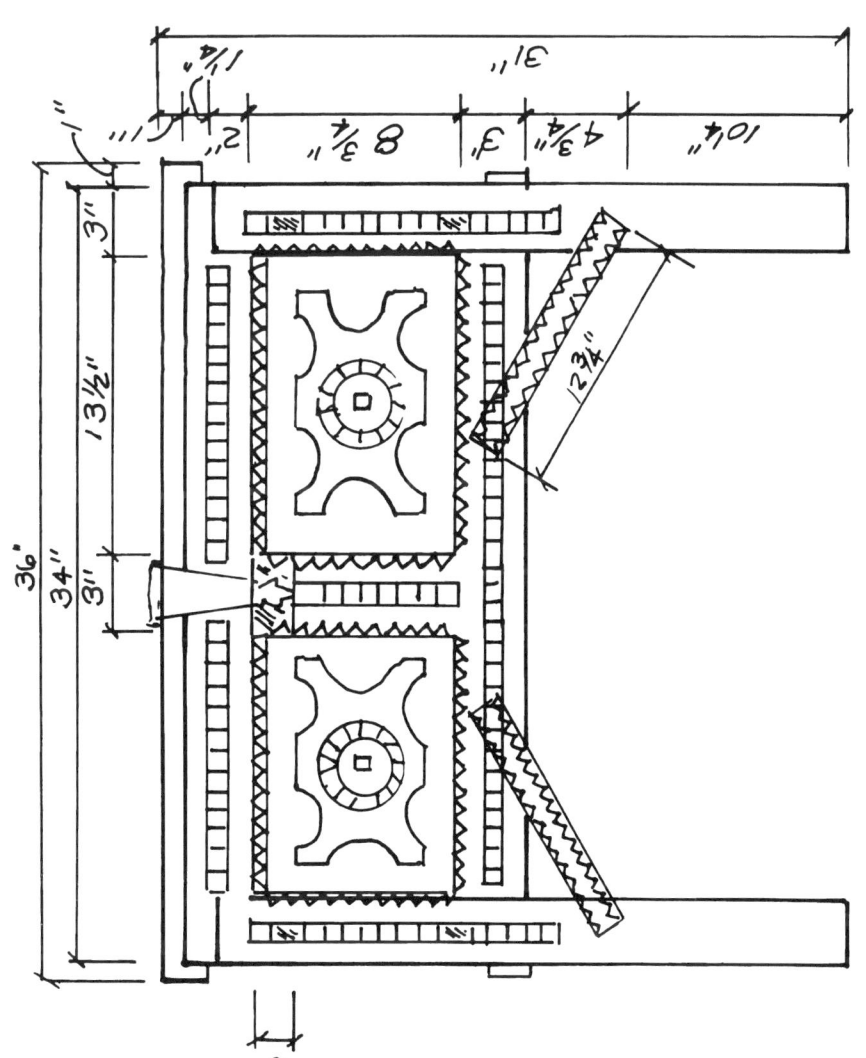

SIDE

FRONT

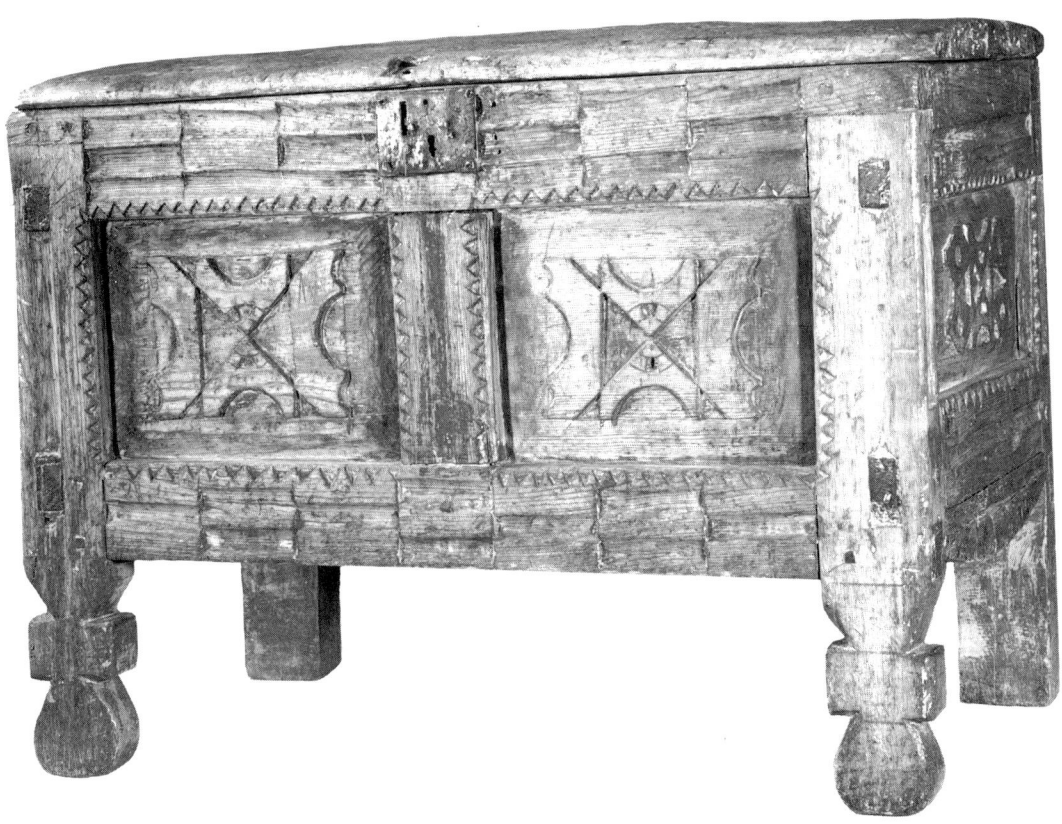

Chest on Cross Legs

THIS EIGHTEENTH- OR early nineteenth-century chest is distinguished by the crosses cut into the profile of its front legs. The top and bottom front rails are relieved by deep, wide, staggered gouge carvings and the inside edges of the rails are cut in a serrated pattern. The bottom is double planked with the outer layer showing a convex shape that mimics the top. *International Folk Art Foundation Collections at the Museum of International Folk Art, Santa Fe, New Mexico (FW-102).*

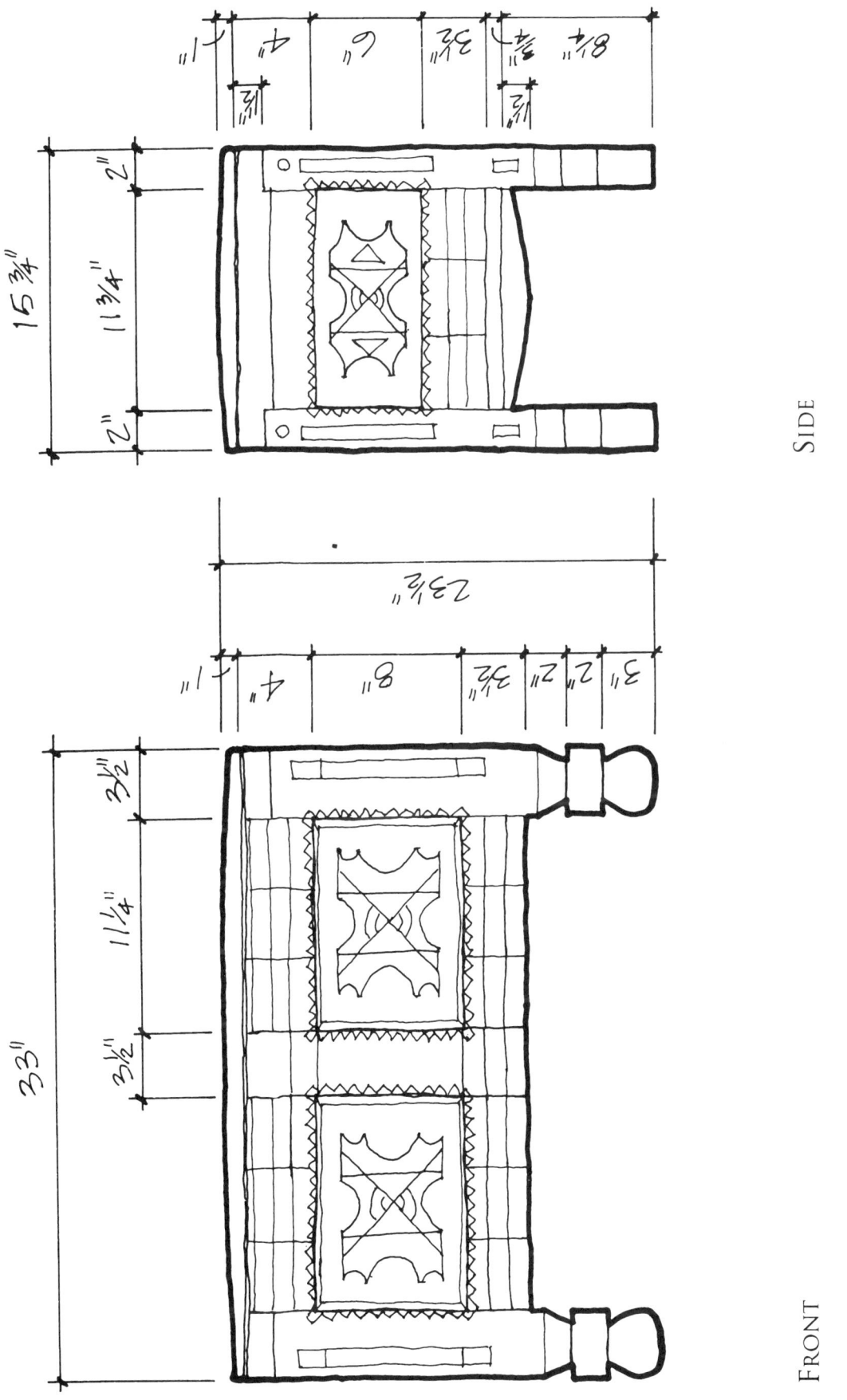

SIDE

FRONT

33

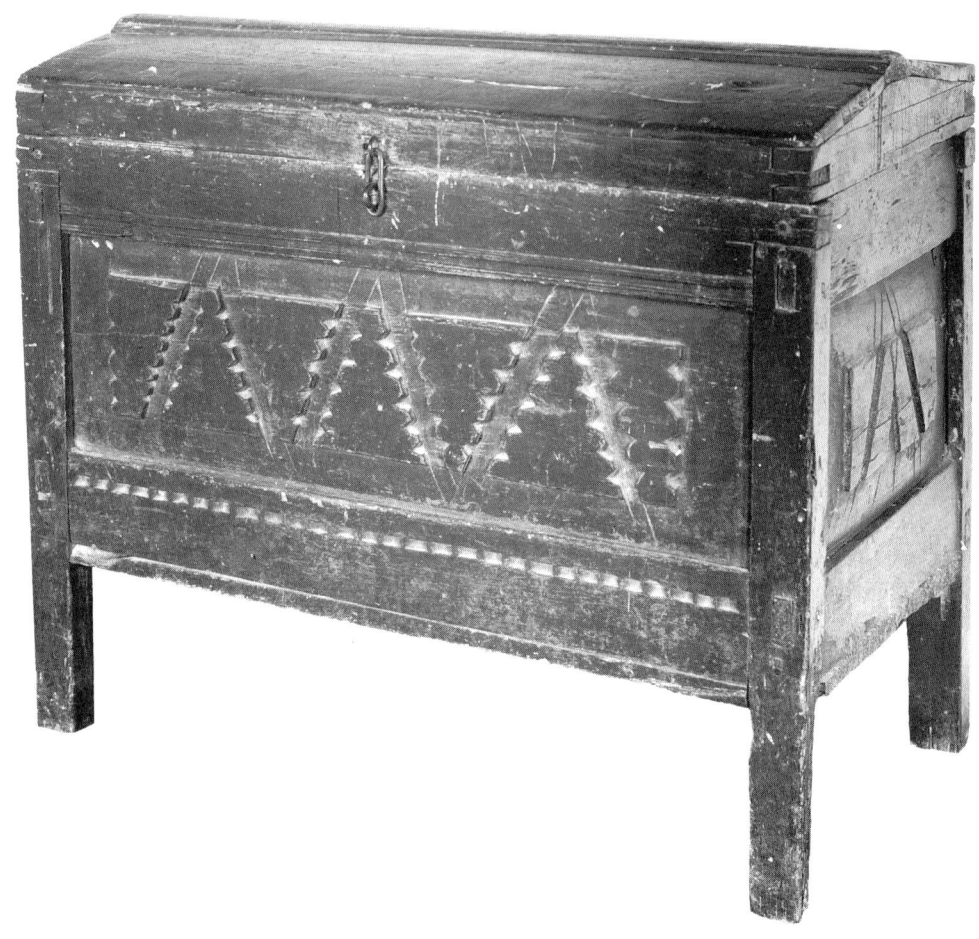

Triangle Chip Carved Chest on Legs

THE EDGES OF the triangles carved in relief in the front raised panel of this chest are further carved with serrated edges. But the edges of similar triangles carved into the side panels are not. The base frame of the top is held together with a single dovetail joint and the raised lid is made from three boards. An overlapping joint holds the top front rail to the legs while the bottom and side rails employ through mortise-and-tenon joints. The bottom of the chest is made up of thin adzed boards nailed to the bottom of the chest's frame. *Collection of the School of American Research, Santa Fe, New Mexico (FW-103).*

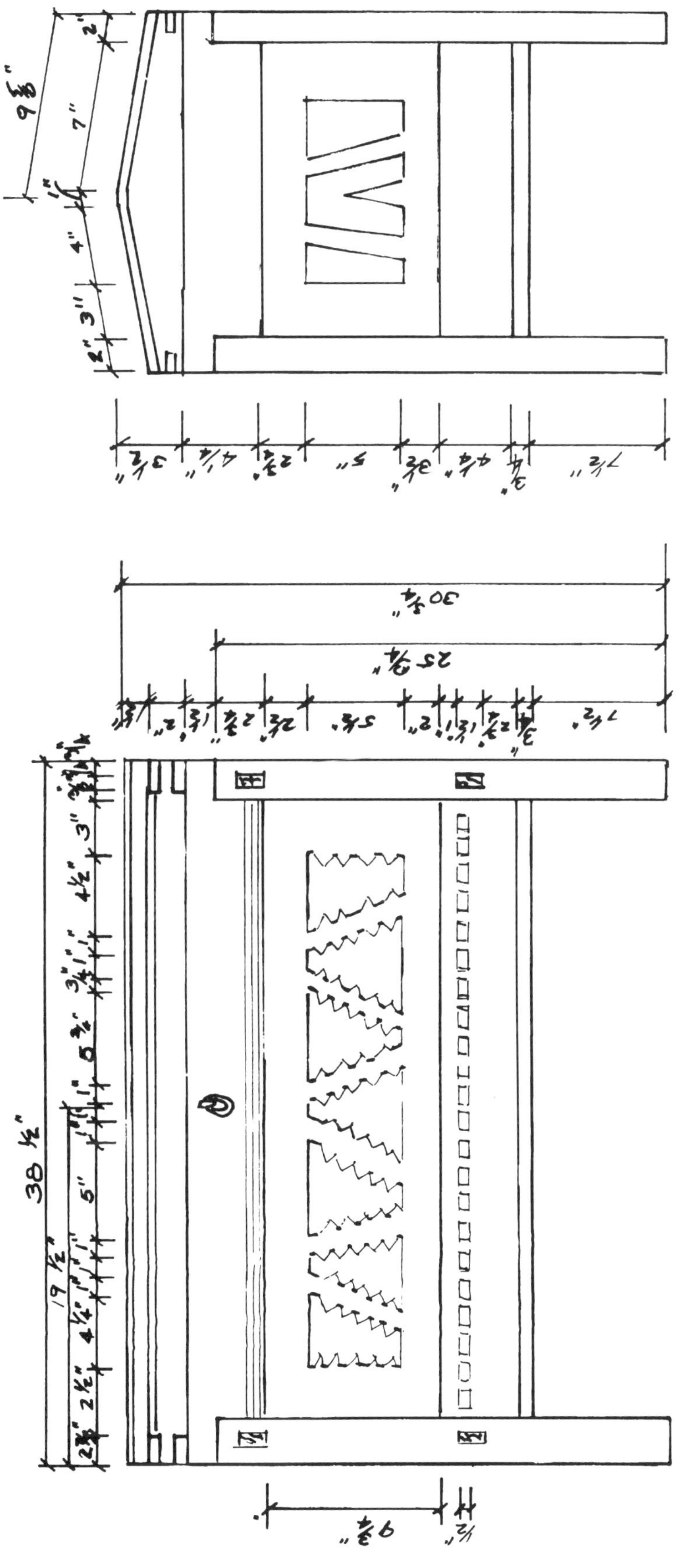

SIDE

FRONT

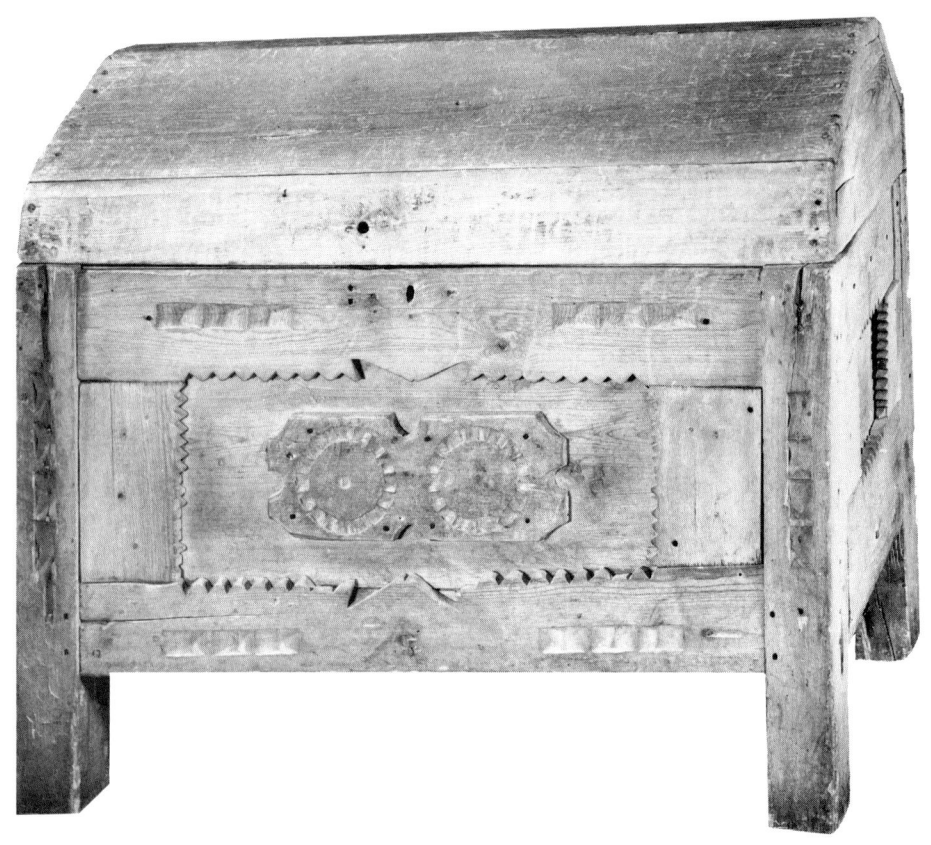

Coffered Lid Appliqué Chest

A POPULAR TECHNIQUE to embellish an otherwise simple chest was to nail elaborately chip carved and cutout boards to its surface to give it a raised panel look. This chest is topped with a five-board coffered lid. *Spanish Colonial Arts Society, Inc. Collection on loan to the Museum of New Mexico, Museum of International Folk Art, Santa Fe, New Mexico (FW-104).*

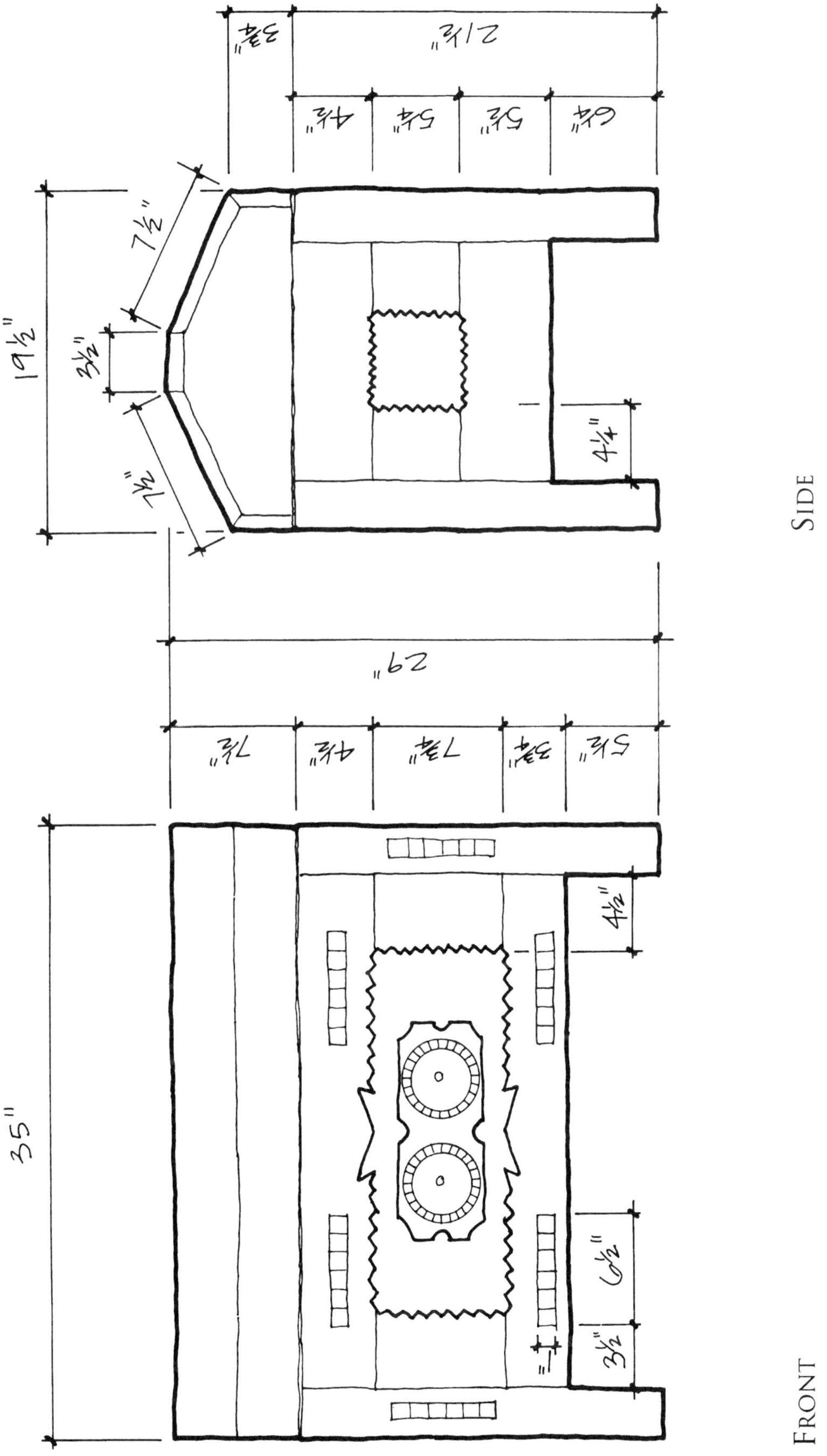

SIDE

21½"

3⅜"
6¼" 5¼" 5¼" 4½"

19½"

7½"

3½"

7½"

4¼"

29"

FRONT

7½"
3⅜" 4½" 7⅜" 3⅜" 5¼"

4½"

35"

6½"

3½"

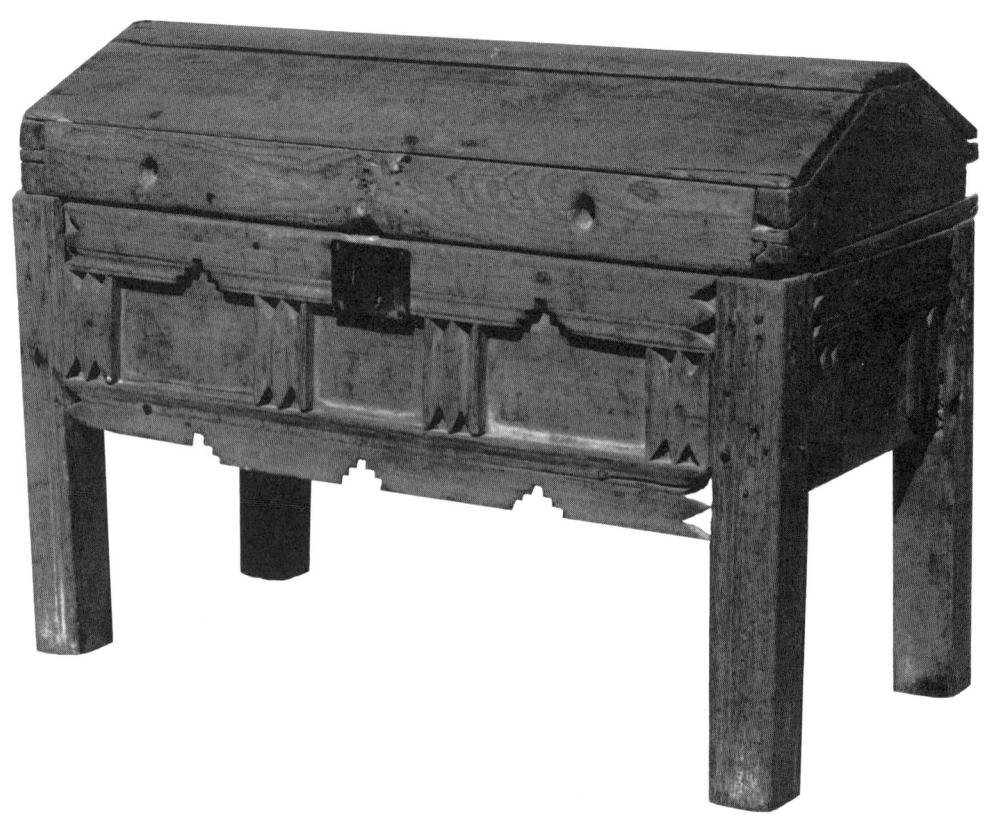

Coffered Lid False Frame Chest

HERE IS A SWEET example of a false frame chest where the delicately cut detail pieces have been fastened to the front of a very plain board box. Two short applique pieces with triangles cut in their ends, similar to those seen on the front of the box, decorate the sides. Notice the step-and-mesa design cut into the longer appliqué pieces along the front panel. The coffered lid is made from three boards nailed to a dovetailed frame. The legs are solid pieces below the bottom of the box that have been cut to wrap around the edges of the box above that point. *Collection of the School of American Research, Santa Fe, New Mexico (FW-105).*

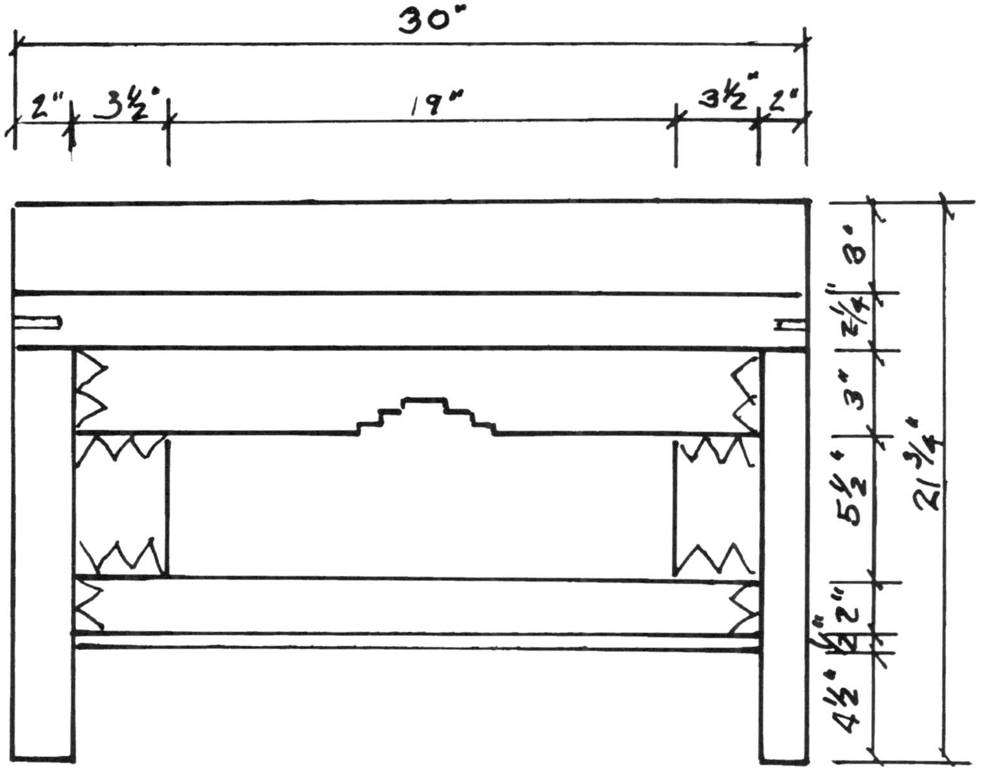

SIDE

FRONT

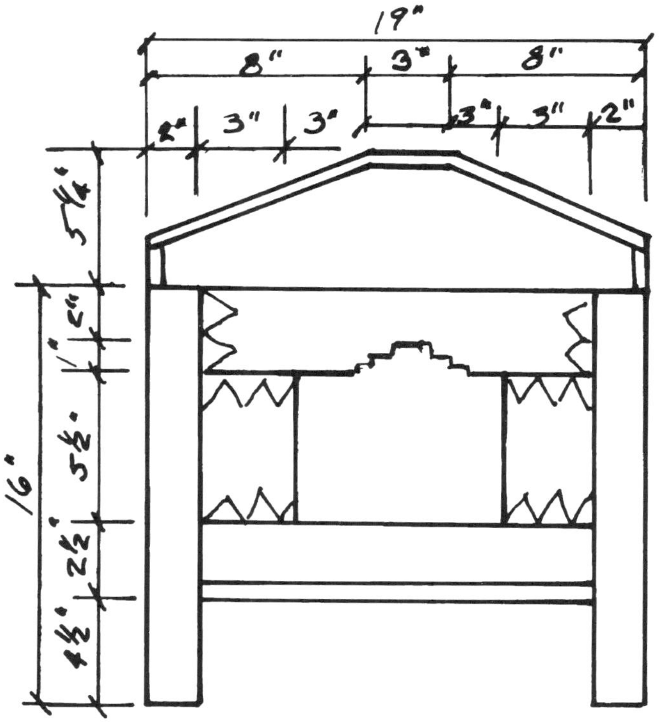

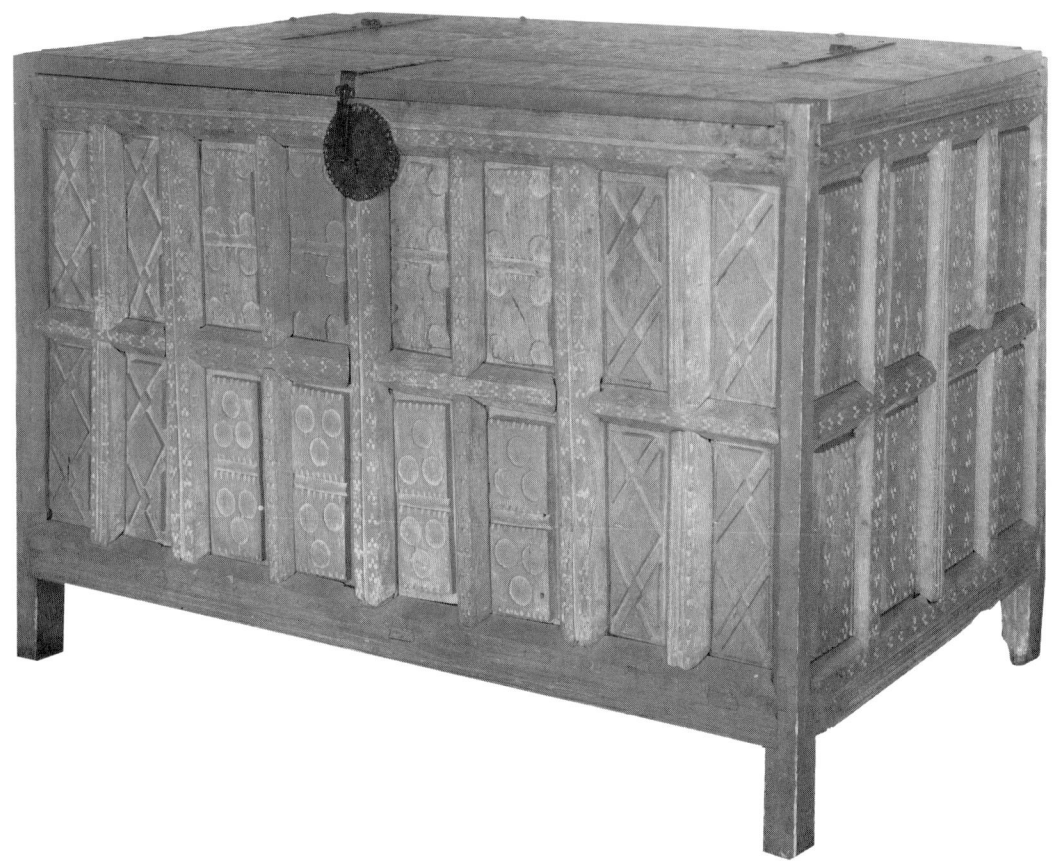

Chip Carved Harinero

WHILE THE TOPS of most harineros are divided into two or three hinged sections to gain access to separate bins below, the top on this one is a single piece made up of three separate boards. The piece is painted red but has dulled over time. The top rail and the panel dividers, both across the front and on the sides, are richly decorated with a small ram's horn type chip carving. Three different carved patterns decorate the front panels: four of the same panel flank the right and left sides of the chest while a second pattern occupies the top middle four panels and a third pattern adorns the four panels below. *Collection of the School of American Research, Santa Fe, New Mexico (FW-106).*

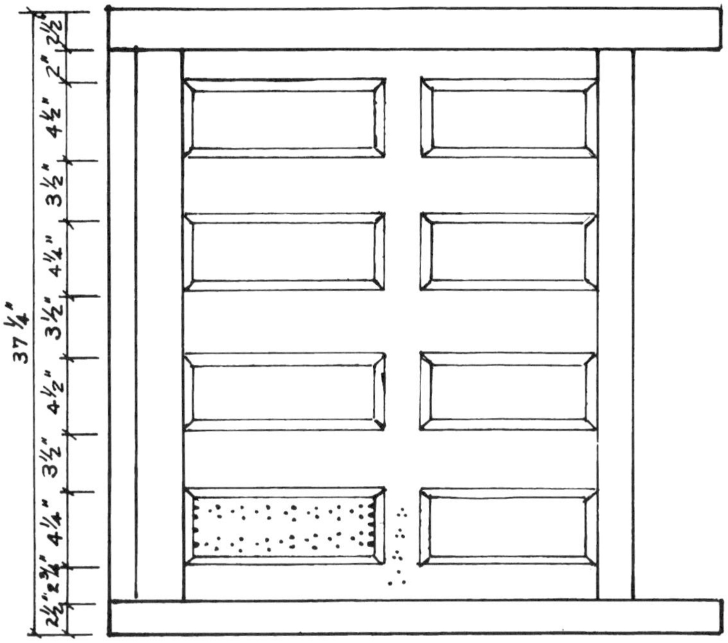

SIDE

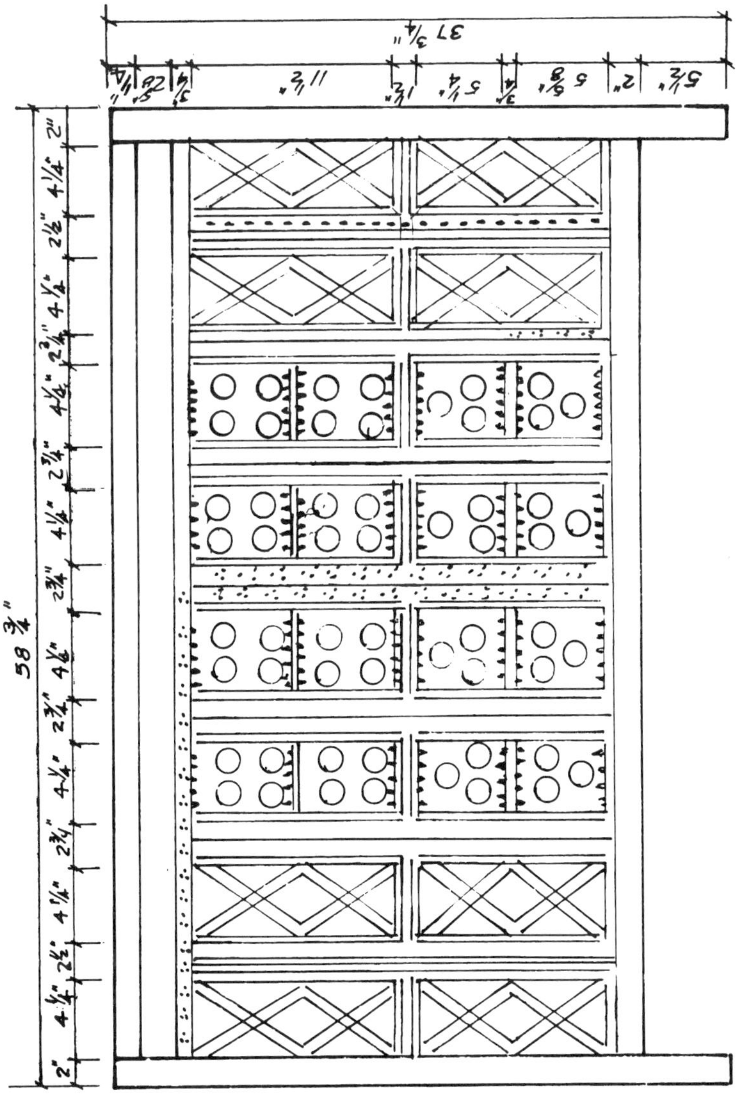

FRONT

41

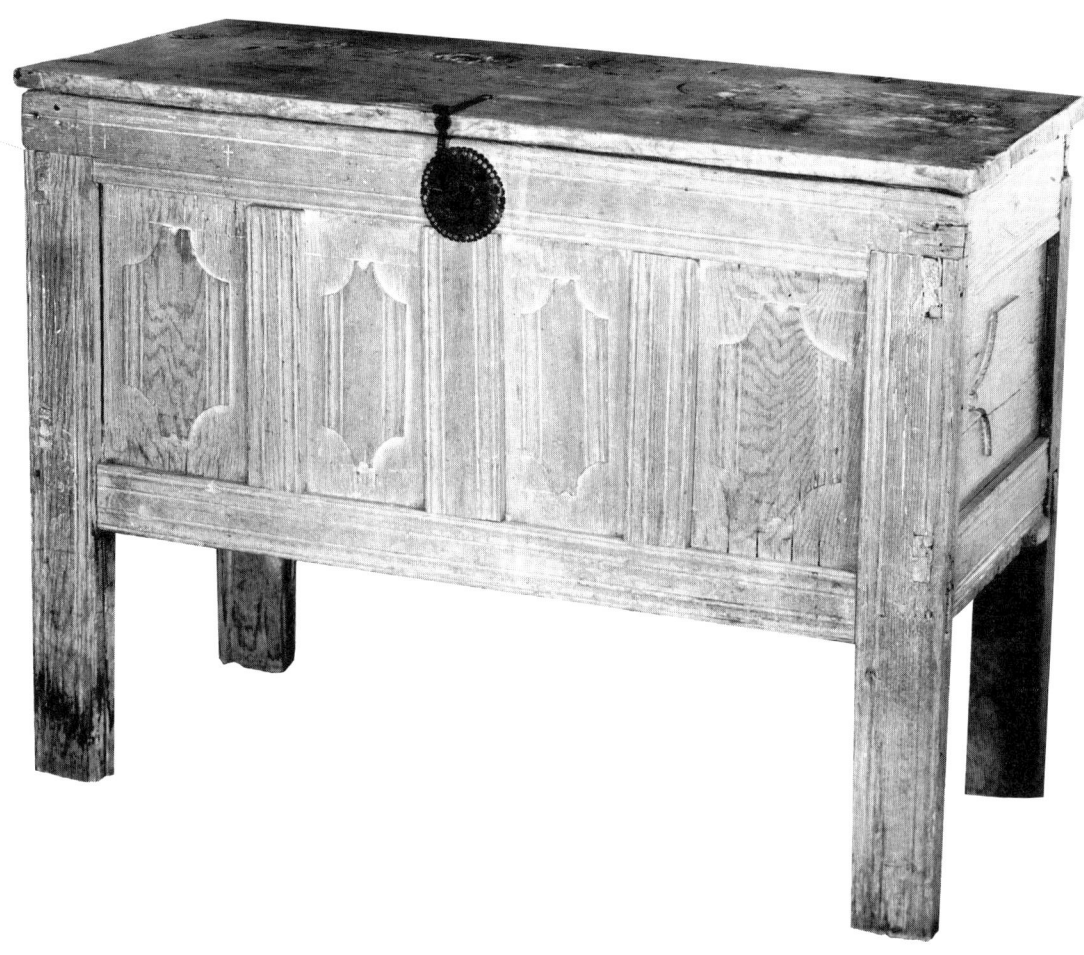

Geometric Carved Chest on Legs

THIS FRAMED LATE-NINETEENTH-CENTURY chest features carved raised panels front and back which float in dados cut into the length of the legs. The top front and back rails are joined to the top of the legs with a half-lap joint while the other rails are joined to the legs with through mortise-and-tenon joints. The rails and legs are decorated with fluted molding lines. The top has an overlapping hasp which fits into a circular lock plate cover. *Spanish Colonial Arts Society, Inc. Collection on loan to the Museum of New Mexico, Museum of International Folk Art, Santa Fe, New Mexico (FW-107).*

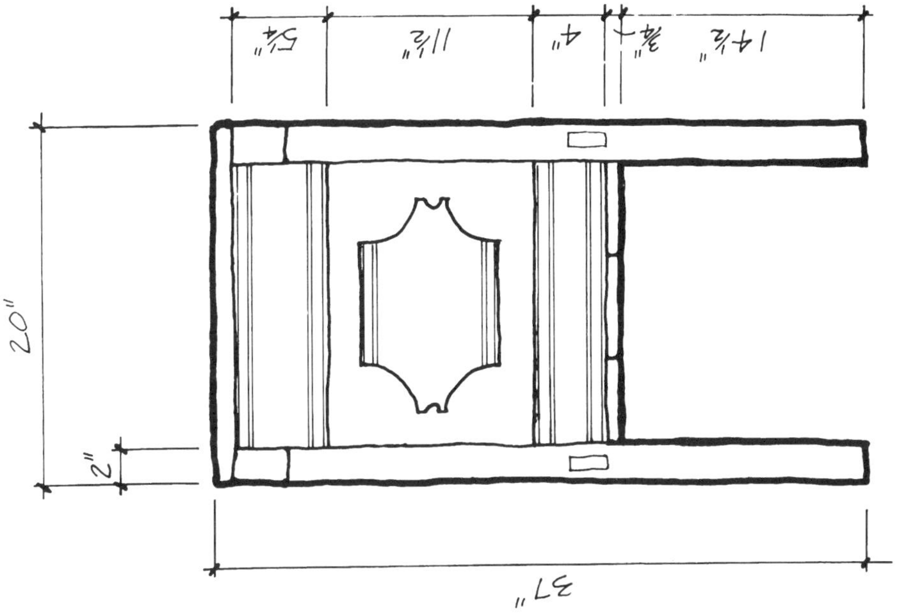

SIDE

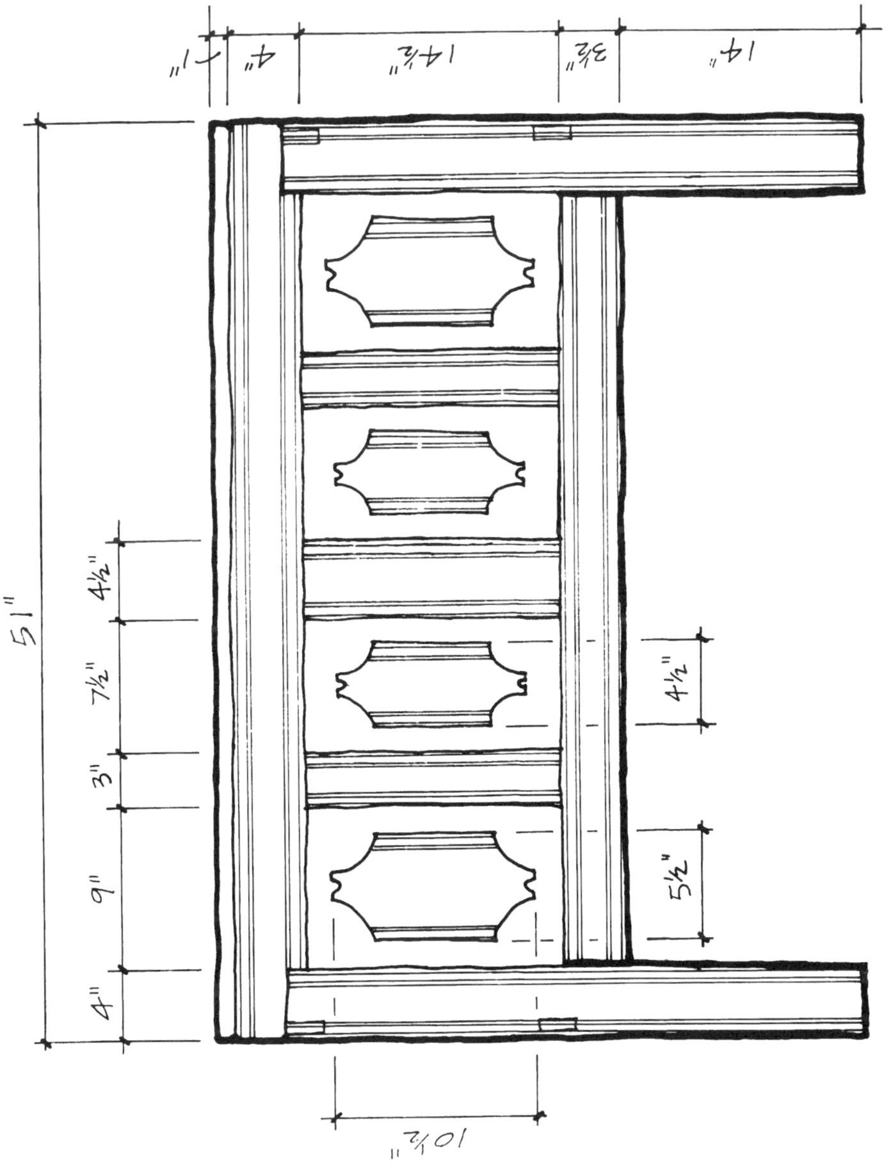

FRONT

43

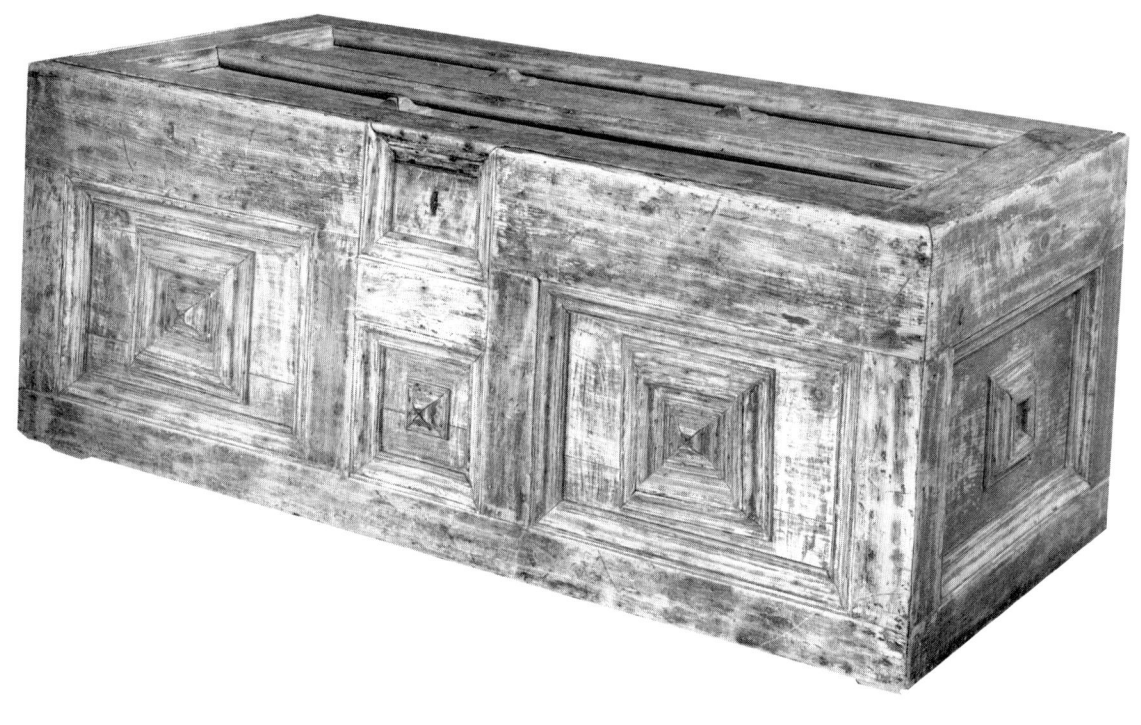

Carpenter's Chest with Molding Framing

HERE IS A simple carpenter's chest that a carpenter made fancy by the creative application of heavy molding set in square patterns with mitered corners on all sides as well as the top. *Spanish Colonial Arts Society, Inc. Collection on loan to the Museum of New Mexico, Museum of International Folk Art, Santa Fe, New Mexico (FW-108).*

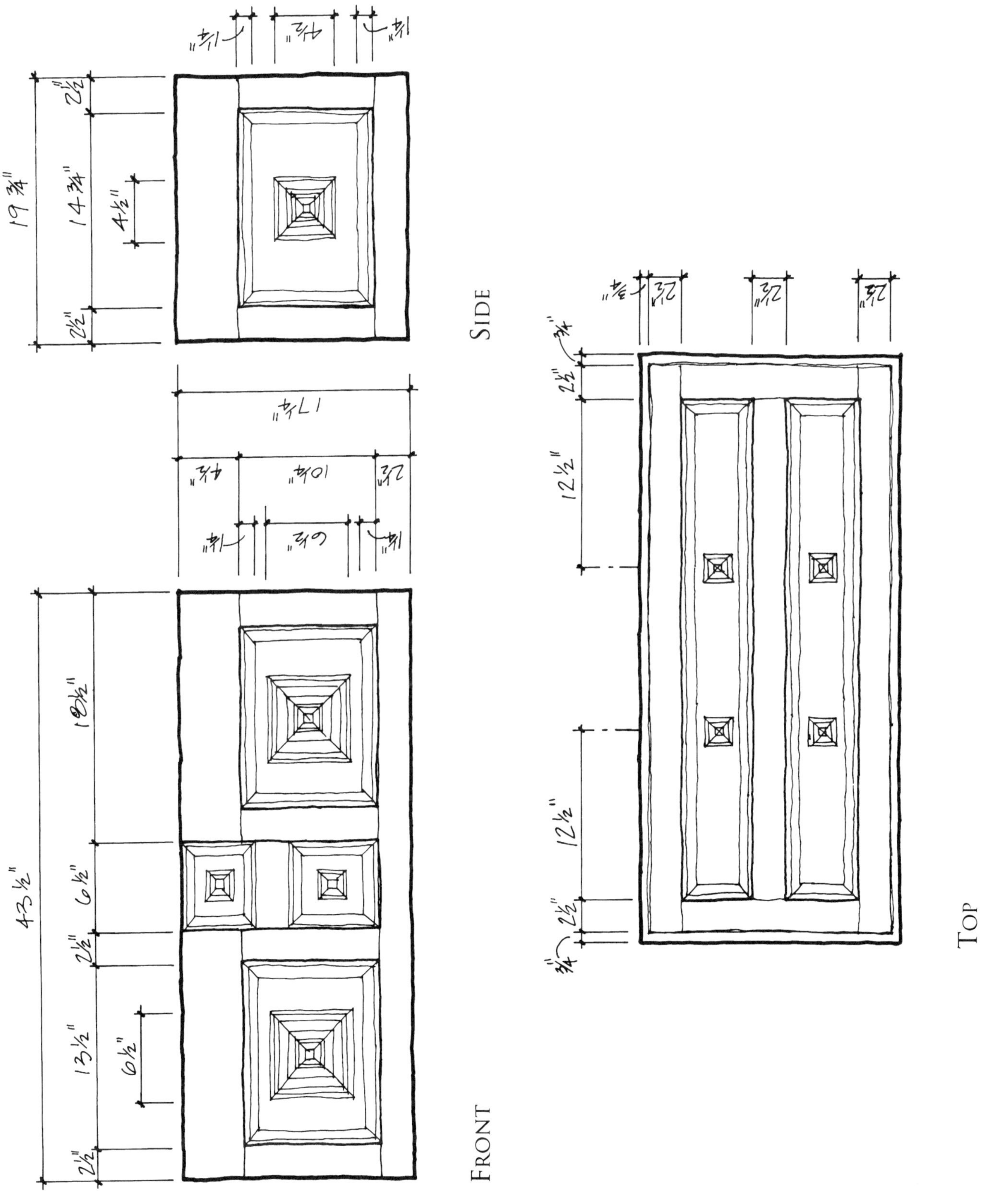

SIDE

FRONT

TOP

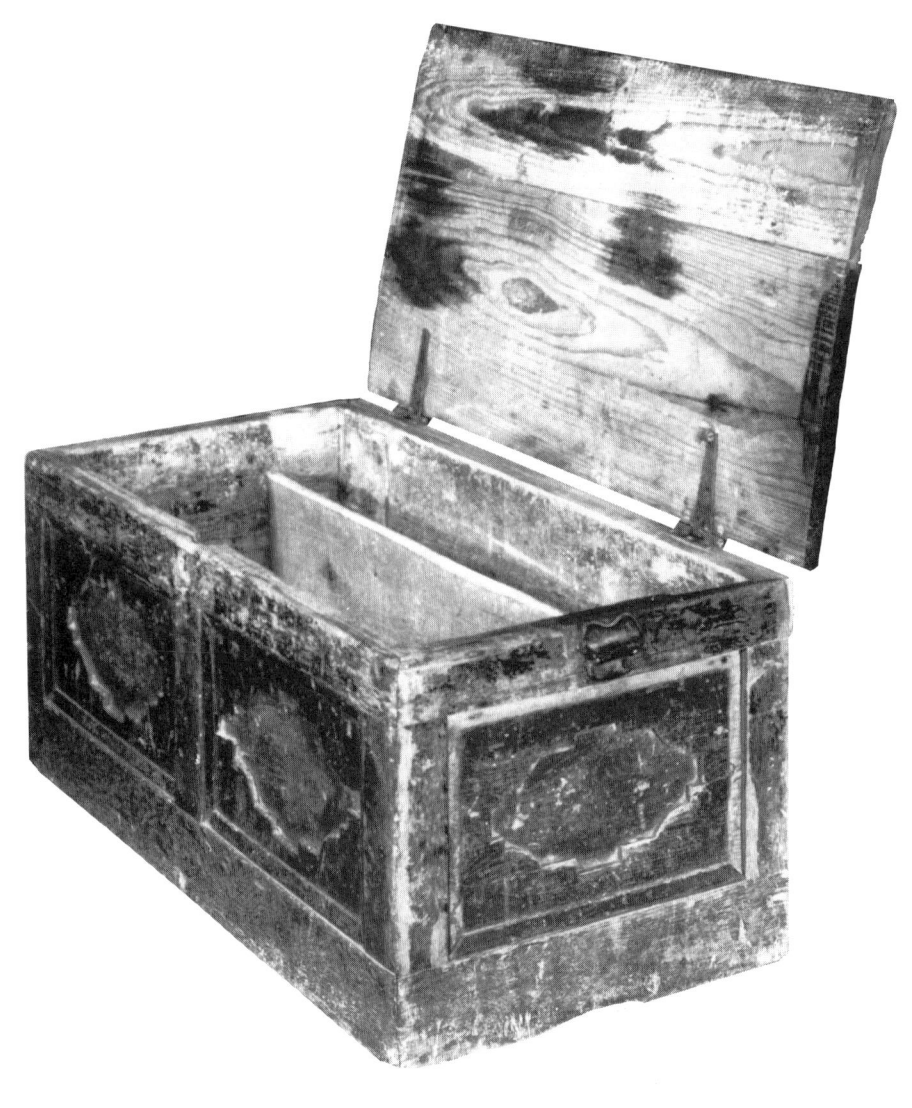

Step-and-Mesa Appliqué Chest

THIS PLAIN CARPENTER'S toolbox was embellished with appliqué panels cut into the step-and-mesa pattern and then trimmed with pieces of plain, flat stock. The interior is divided into two compartments. The appliqué panels are painted green while the box sides beneath are red. *Museum of New Mexico Collections, Museum of International Folk Art, Santa Fe, New Mexico (FW-109).*

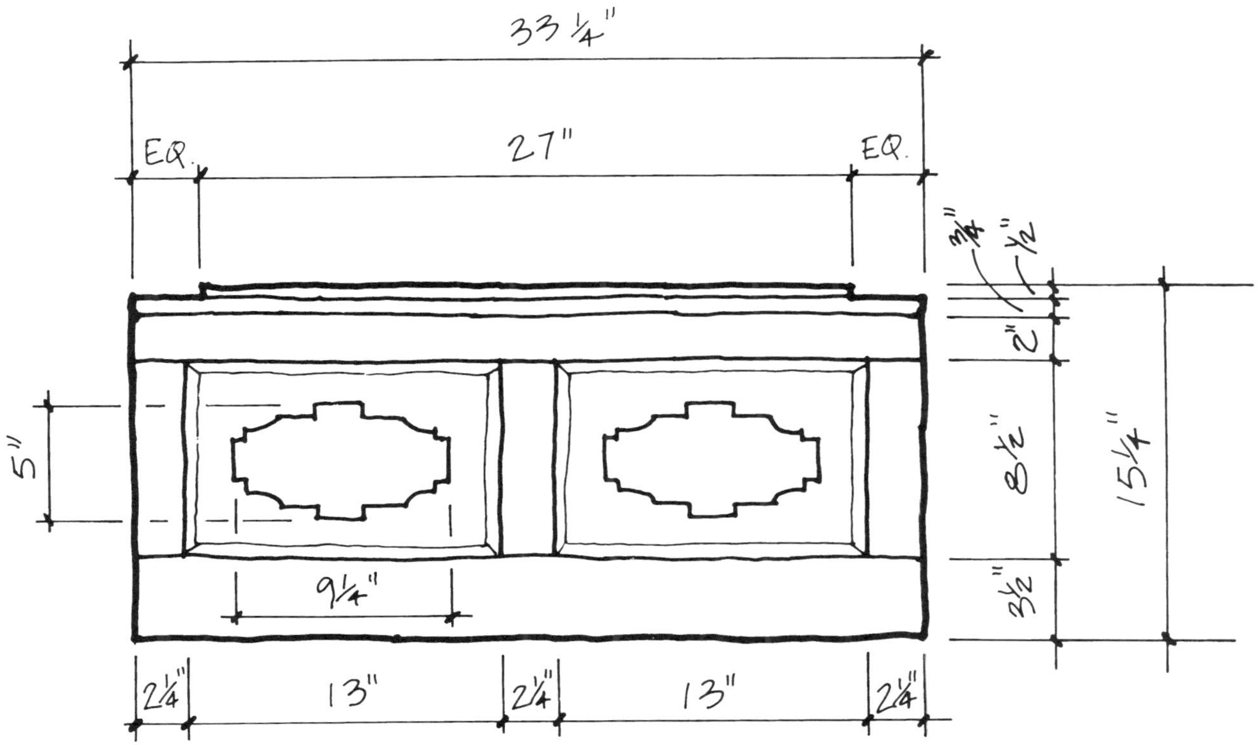

17½"

11½"

E.Q.

E.Q.

2"

13½"

2"

SIDE

15¼"

3¼"

2"

8½"

3¼"

33¼"

27"

E.Q.

E.Q.

2¼"

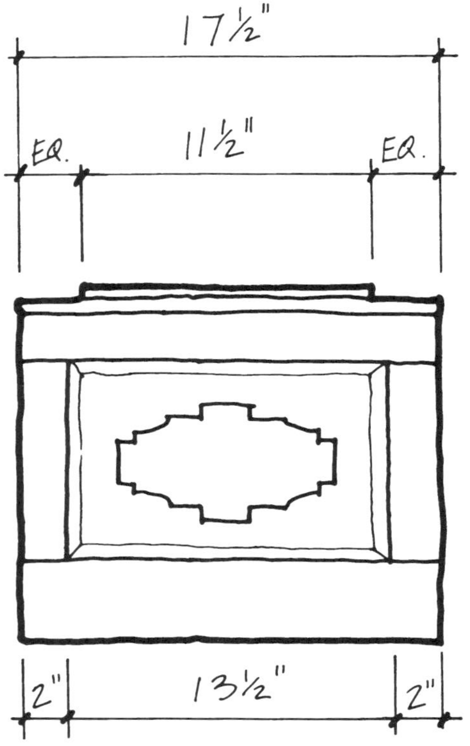

13"

2¼"

13"

2¼"

9¼"

5"

FRONT

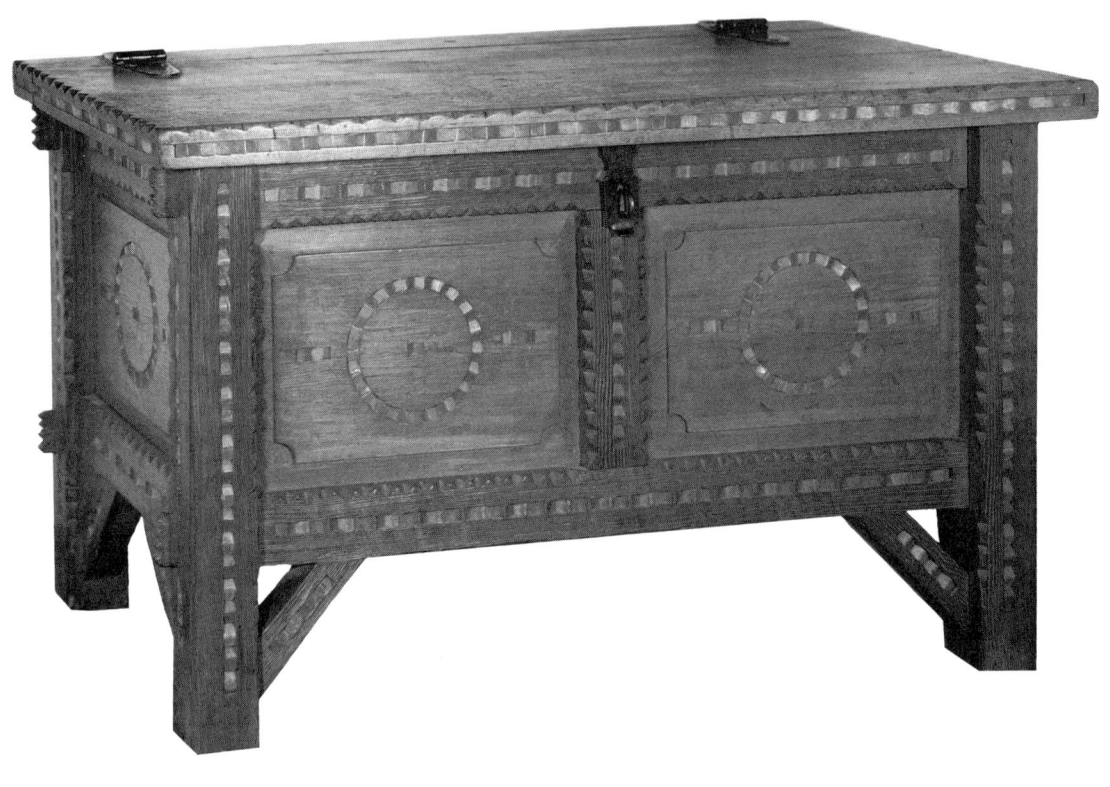

Chip Carved Pueblo Revival/Mission Chest

JESSE NUSSBAUM DESIGNED this chest (along with the chair — p. 74 — and the sideboard — p. 90) as part of an ensemble for the Women's Board Room of the Museum of Fine Arts which opened in 1917. Its protruding tenons reflect the Mission style then popular while the diagonal leg braces and elaborate chip carving echo chests built at least one hundred years earlier. Its lid is hinged to a 3-inch piece that's fixed to the back of the top. The entire box is heavily decorated with sawtooth and basket weave carving where the alternating chips are painted red and blue. *Museum of New Mexico Collections, Museum of International Folk Art, Santa Fe, New Mexico (FW-110).*

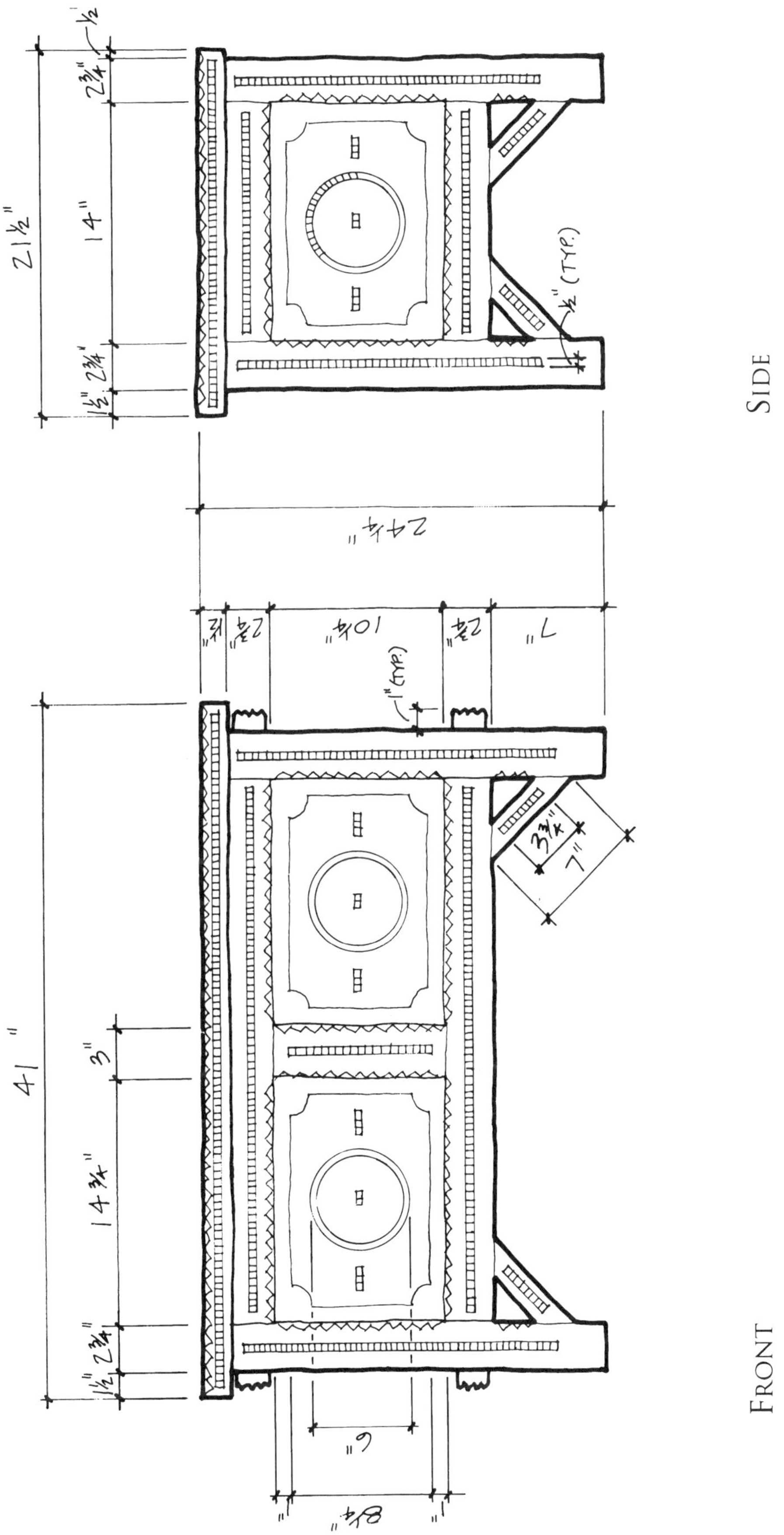

21½"

½

2¾"

14"

½ 2¾"

24¼"

3¼"

2¾"

10¼"

2¾"

7"

1" (TYP.)

½" (TYP.)

3¾"

7"

41"

3"

14¾"

½ 2¾"

6"

8¼"

SIDE

FRONT

49

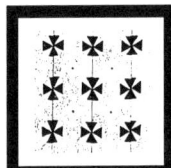

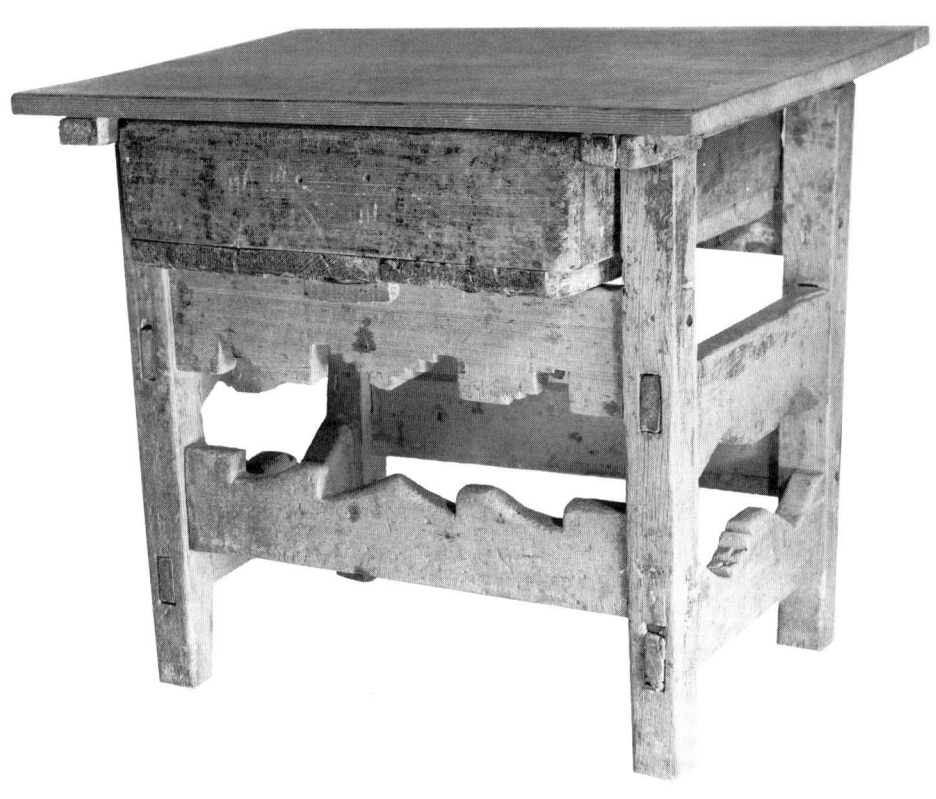

"M" Design End Table

The top and bottom front stretchers on this table form a large "M" design. Notice that the top rail is further cut with four small steps. The side rails have large step-and-mesa style cutouts while the back rails are plain. The drawer slides on the top edge of the top rail and has a small carved finger pull nailed to the bottom planks of the drawer. The table looks as though it might once have been painted a dark reddish brown, and the top is clearly of more recent vintage than the base. *Collection of the School of American Research, Santa Fe, New Mexico (FW-111).*

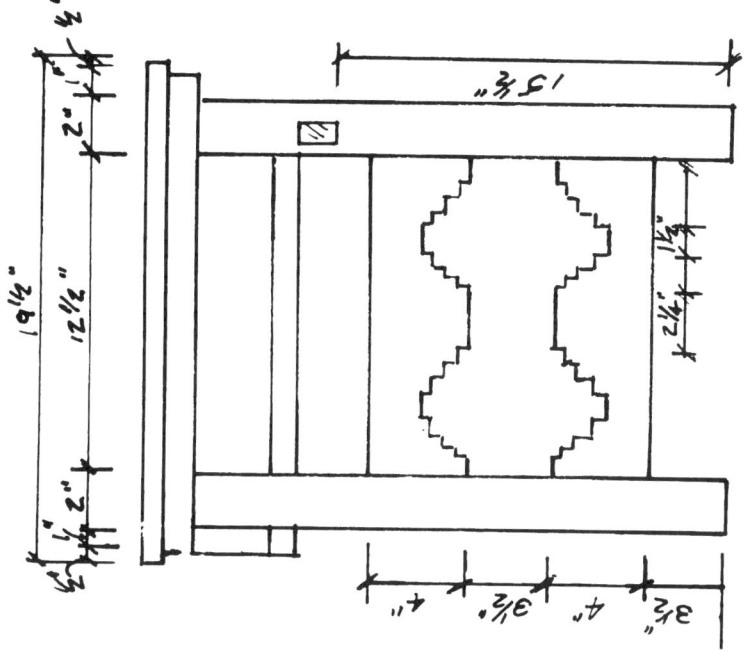

SIDE

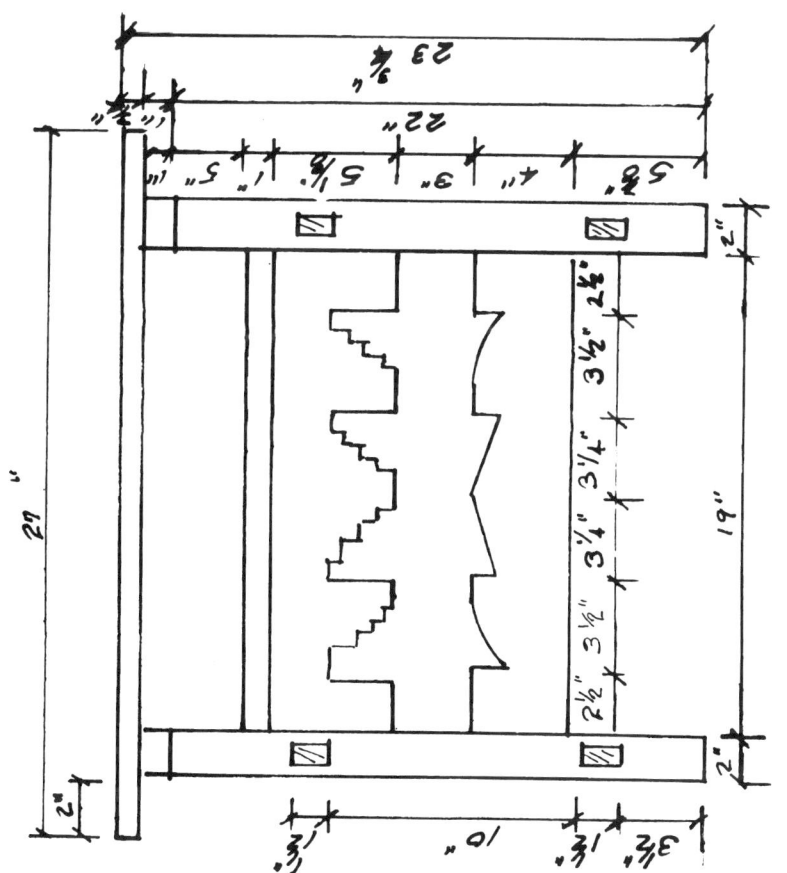

FRONT

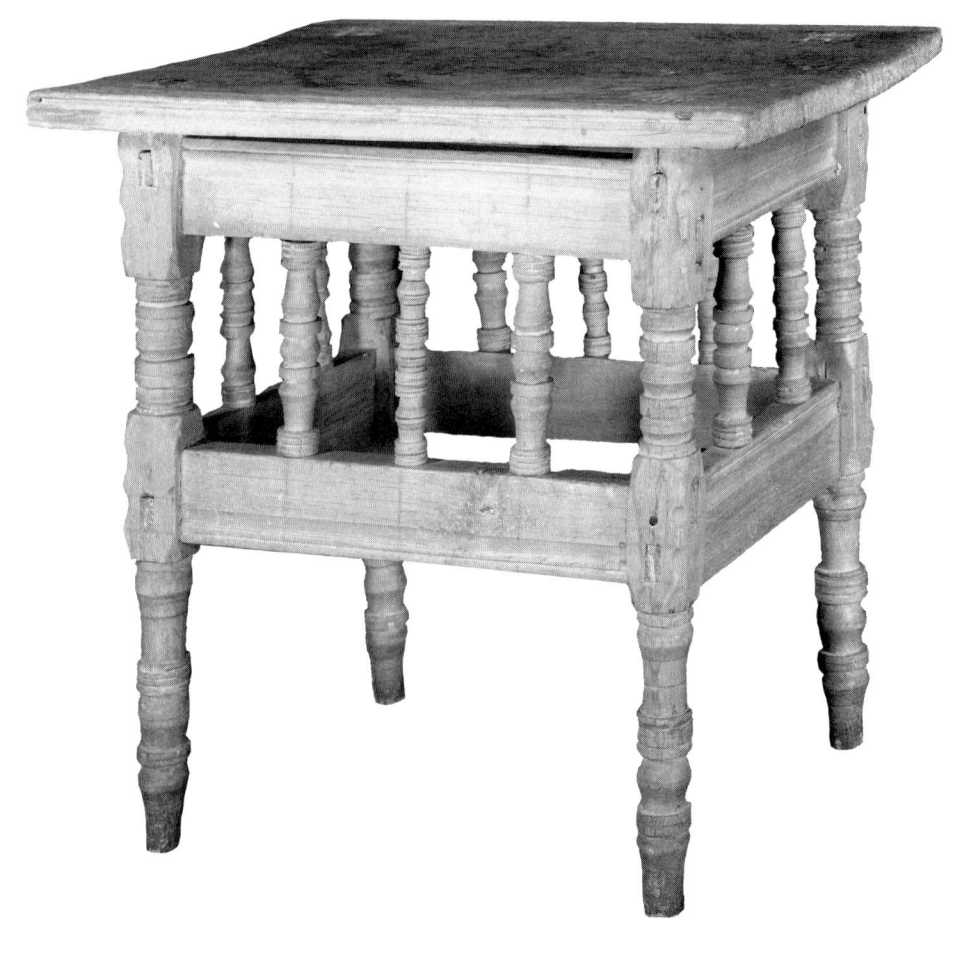

Rectangular Table with Turned Spindles

THE HEAVY BEAD carving visible on the top and bottom edges of the top and bottom side rails, respectively, is repeated the length of the long edges and on the surface of the top piece of this midnineteenth-century table. The top and bottom rails are separated by evenly spaced turned spindles. *Collection of the School of American Research on loan to the Museum of New Mexico, Santa Fe, New Mexico (FW-112).*

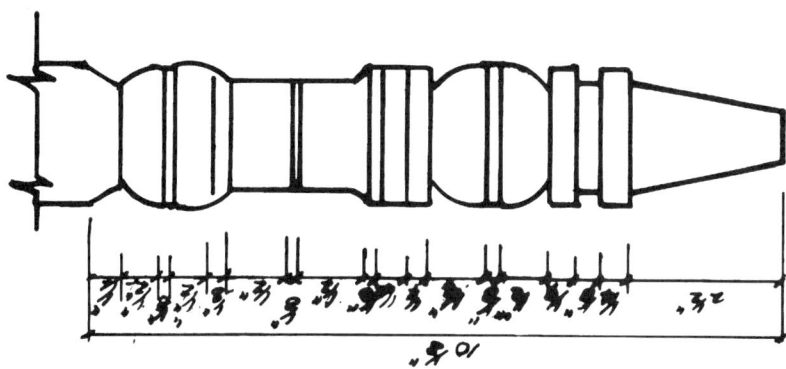

LOWER LEG

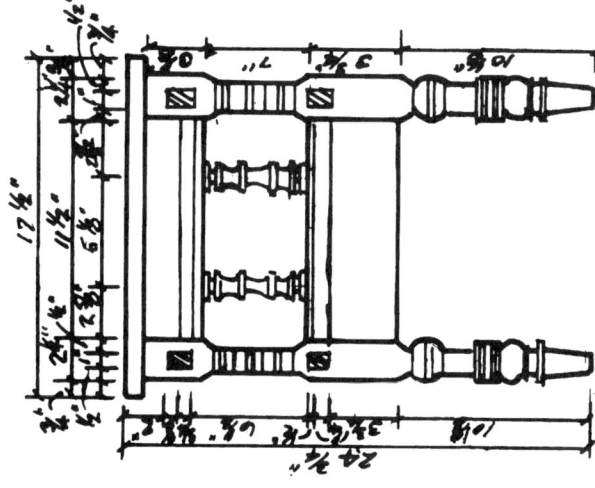

SIDE

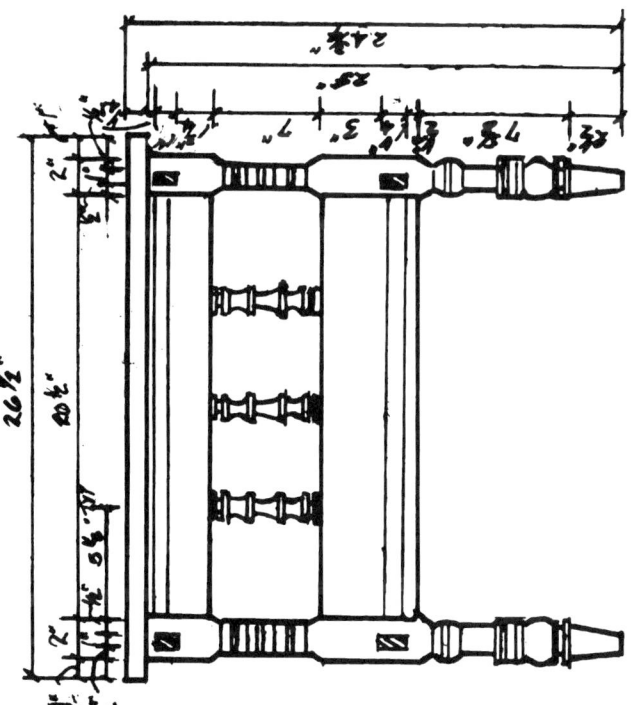

FRONT

53

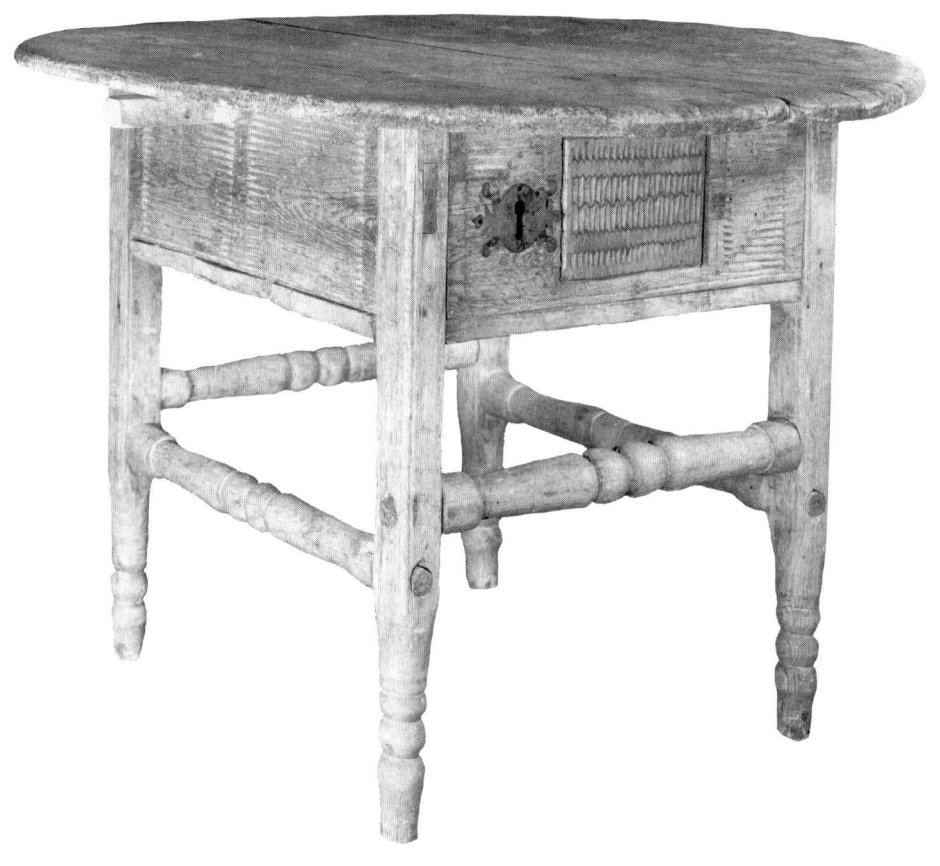

Carved Round-top Table

THE TWO HALVES of the round top on this nineteenth-century table are supported by a rectangular piece of stock let into the skirts on either side and run perpendicular to the gap where the halves are joined. The top is decorated with three concentric circles of small profile gouge carving. While three of the skirts show a similar gouge carving pattern, the fourth is interrupted by a door which opens on pintle hinges that has a purely ornamental lock. *Gift of the Historical Society of New Mexico to the Museum of New Mexico, Museum of International Folk Art, Santa Fe, New Mexico (FW-113).*

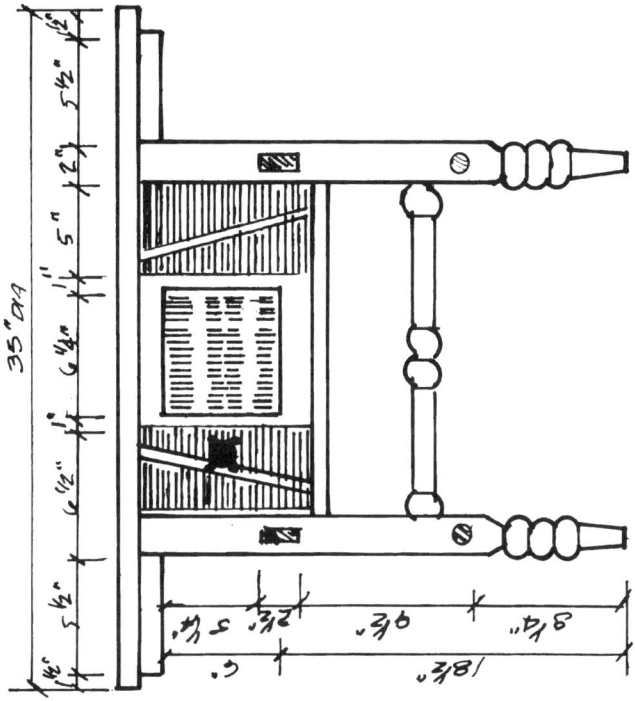

S<small>IDE</small>

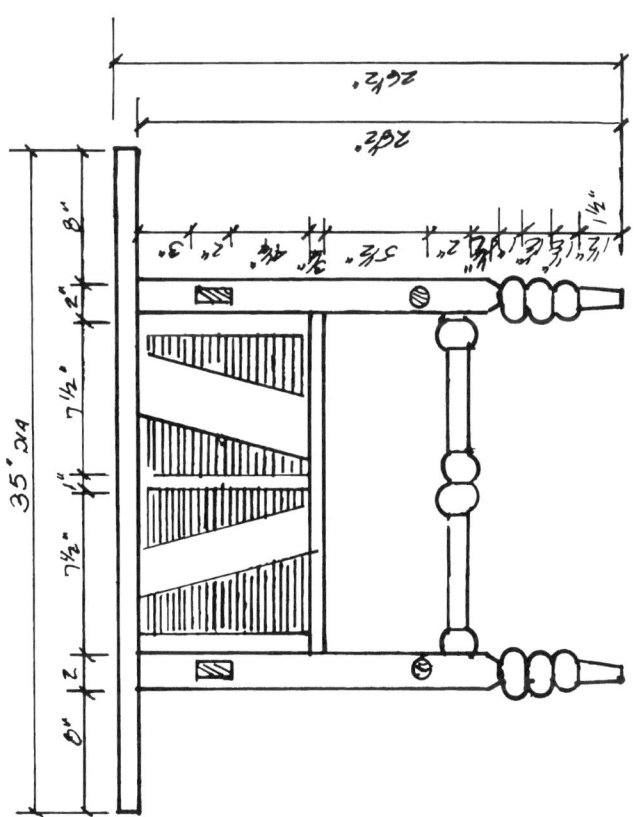

F<small>RONT</small>

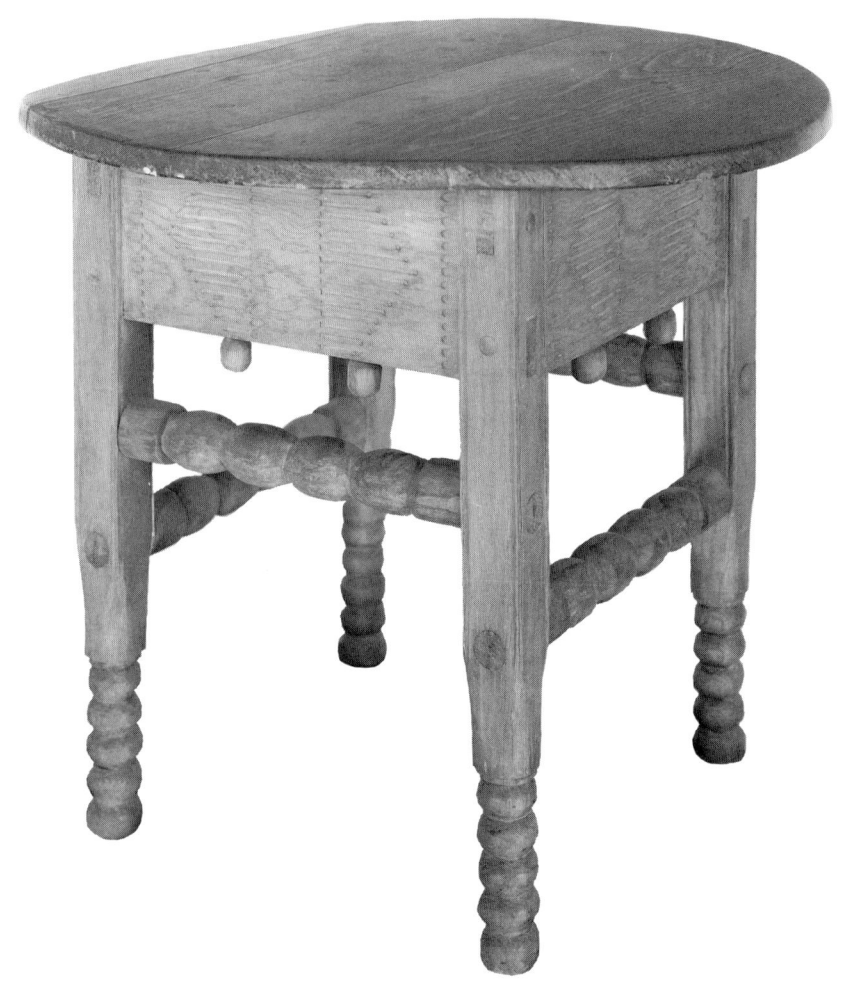

Round-top Table with Turned Legs

THIS TABLE IS quite similar to the previous one (see p. 54) with several key exceptions. There is no door in the apron. Two small balls decorate the bottom of each apron piece. A single bead runs down the side of each corner of each leg. And the legs end in five equal turnings. *Collection of the School of American Research, Santa Fe, New Mexico (FW-114).*

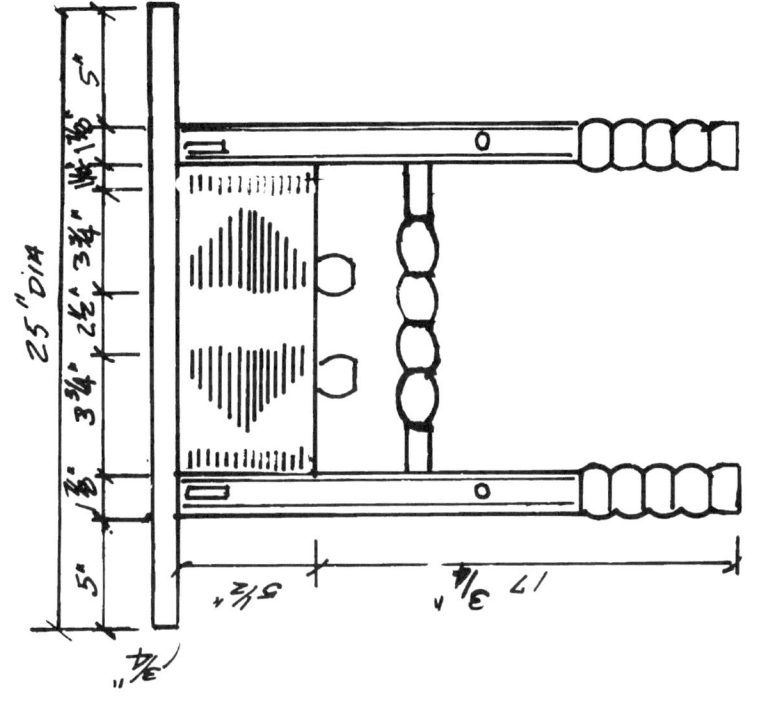

SIDE

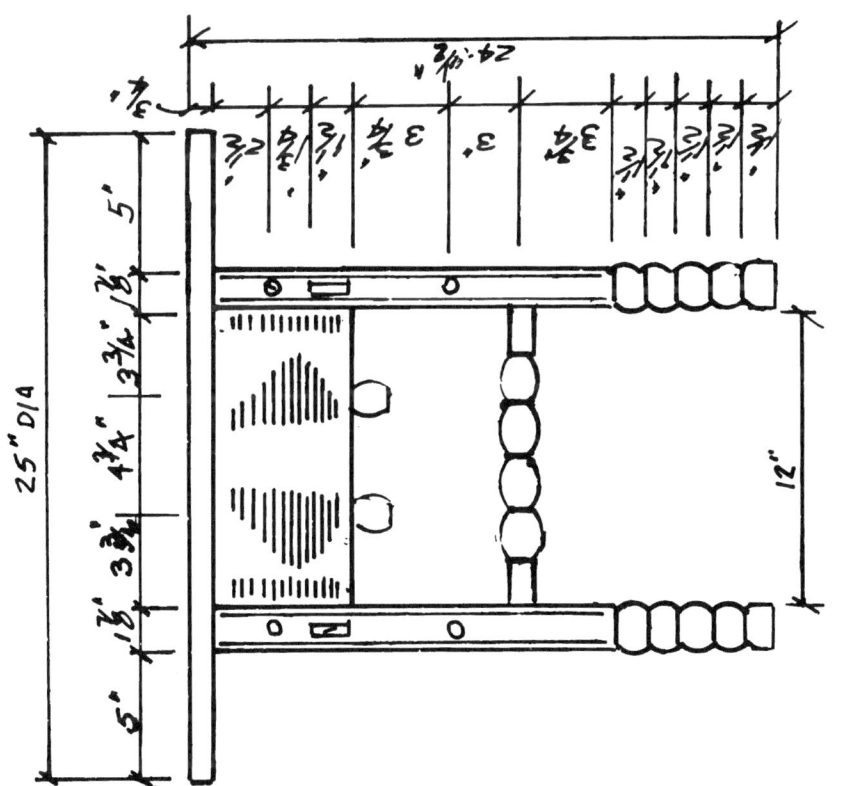

FRONT

57

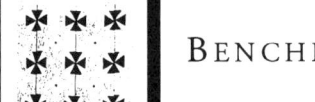

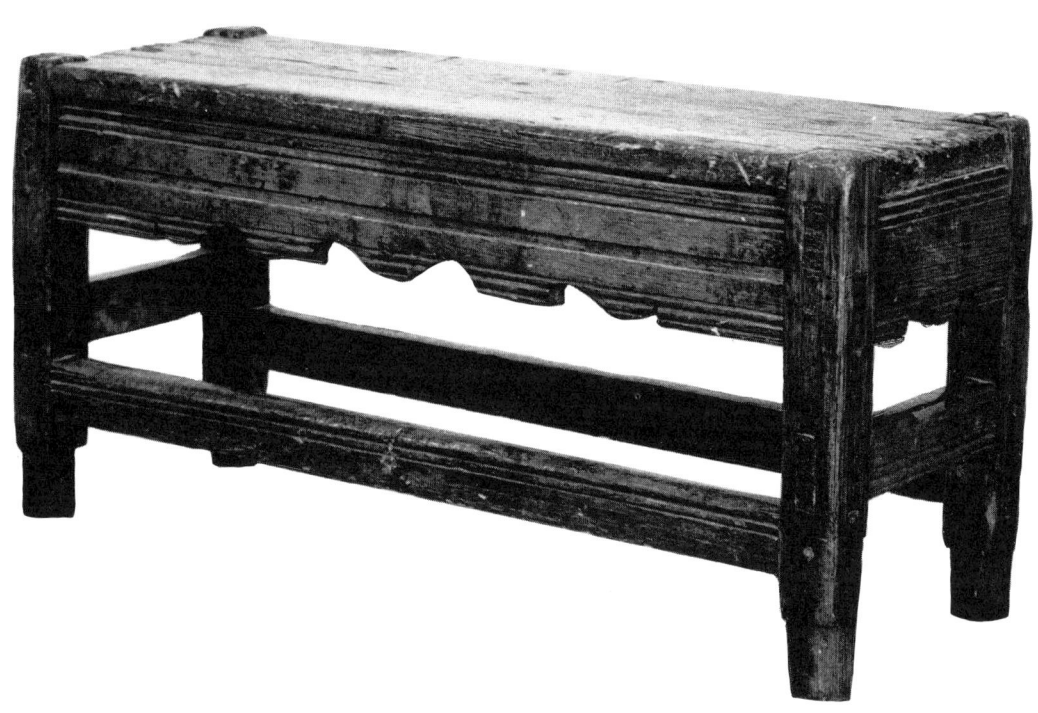

Tarima with "M" Design

THE TARIMA WAS the TV table of its day, a low, tablelike stool on which the woman of the home might serve the meal. This one has delicate beading top and bottom on both side rails, along the front apron, and along the top of the bottom front rail. It has a shallow square groove that runs the length of the center of the front apron. The legs extend above the apron and slightly above the surface of the seat, which is notched around the legs. The bottom of the tarima's legs are rounded up to about 1 1/2 inches off the floor. *Loan of Mrs. Cornelia G. Thompson to the Museum of New Mexico, Museum of International Folk Art, Santa Fe, New Mexico. Photo by David Hart (FW-115).*

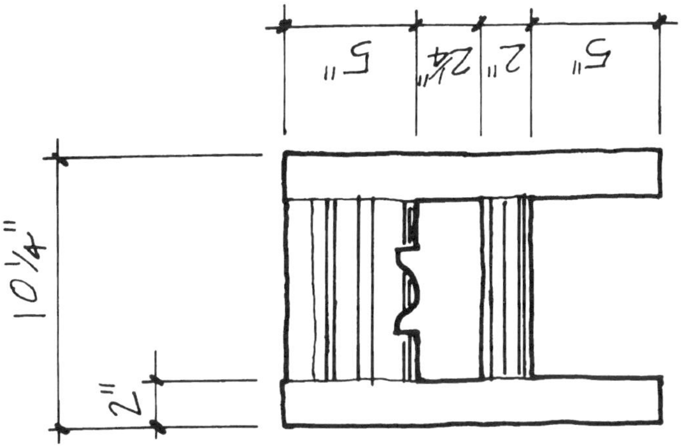

SIDE

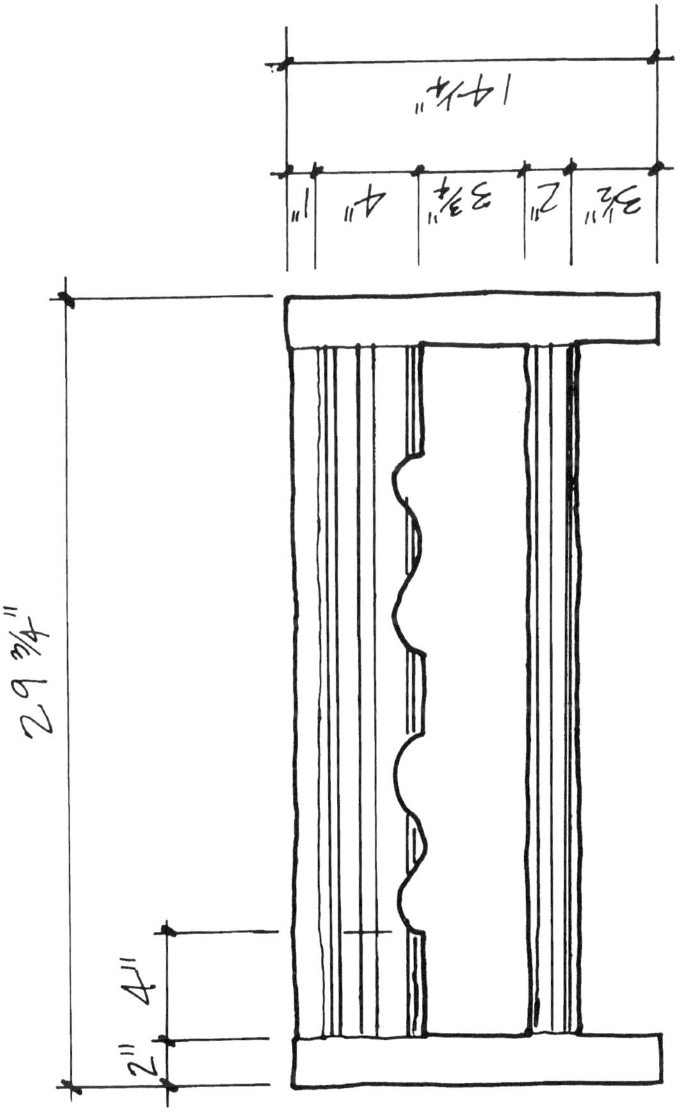

5" 2¼" 2" 5"

10¾"

2"

14½"

2½" 2" 3¾" 4" 1"

29¾"

2" 4"

FRONT

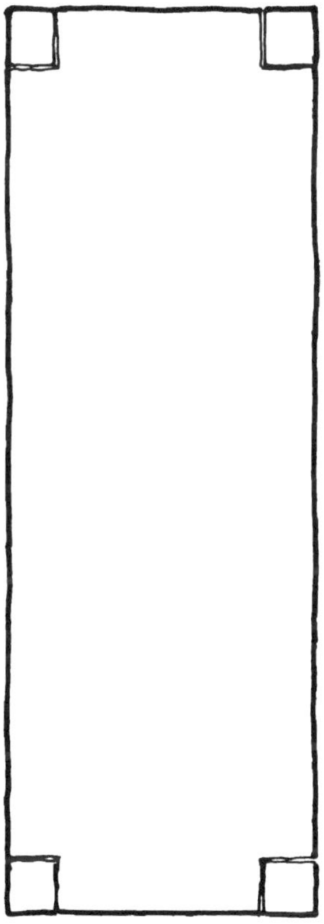

TOP

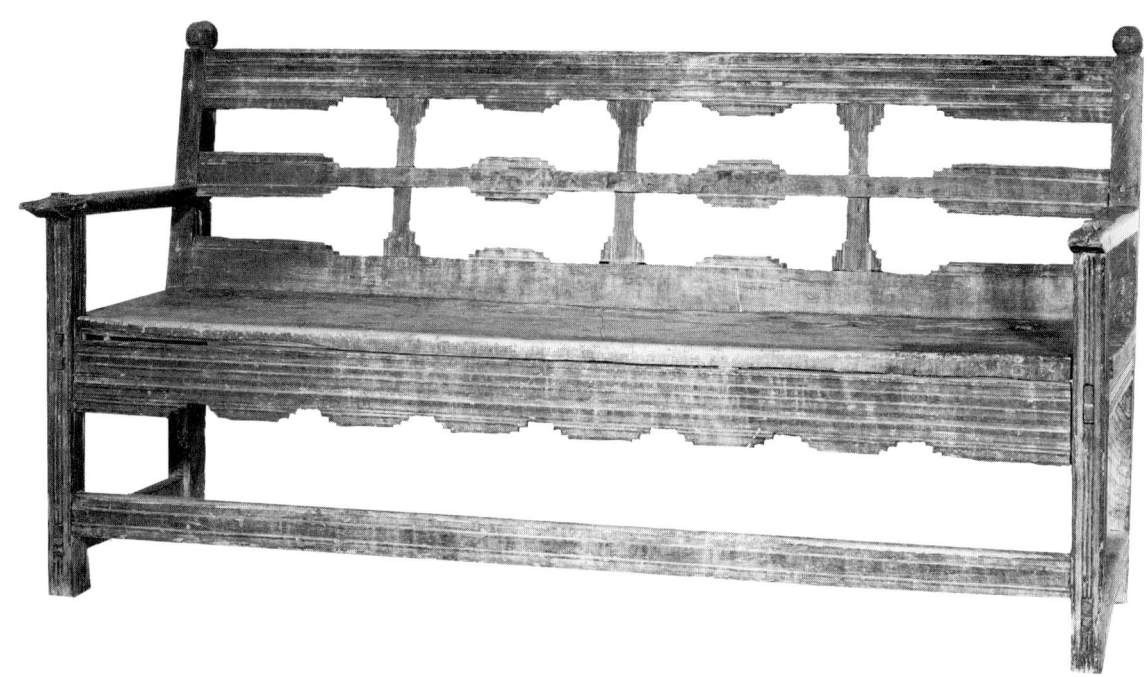

Bench with Ball Finials

THE CENTER BACK rail of this nineteenth-century church pew bench is fastened to the three vertical splats with half-lap joints. The legs are topped with carved ball finials. Prominent on the beaded back and seat rails is the step motif. *Collection of the Museum of International Folk Art, Museum of New Mexico, Santa Fe, New Mexico (FW-116).*

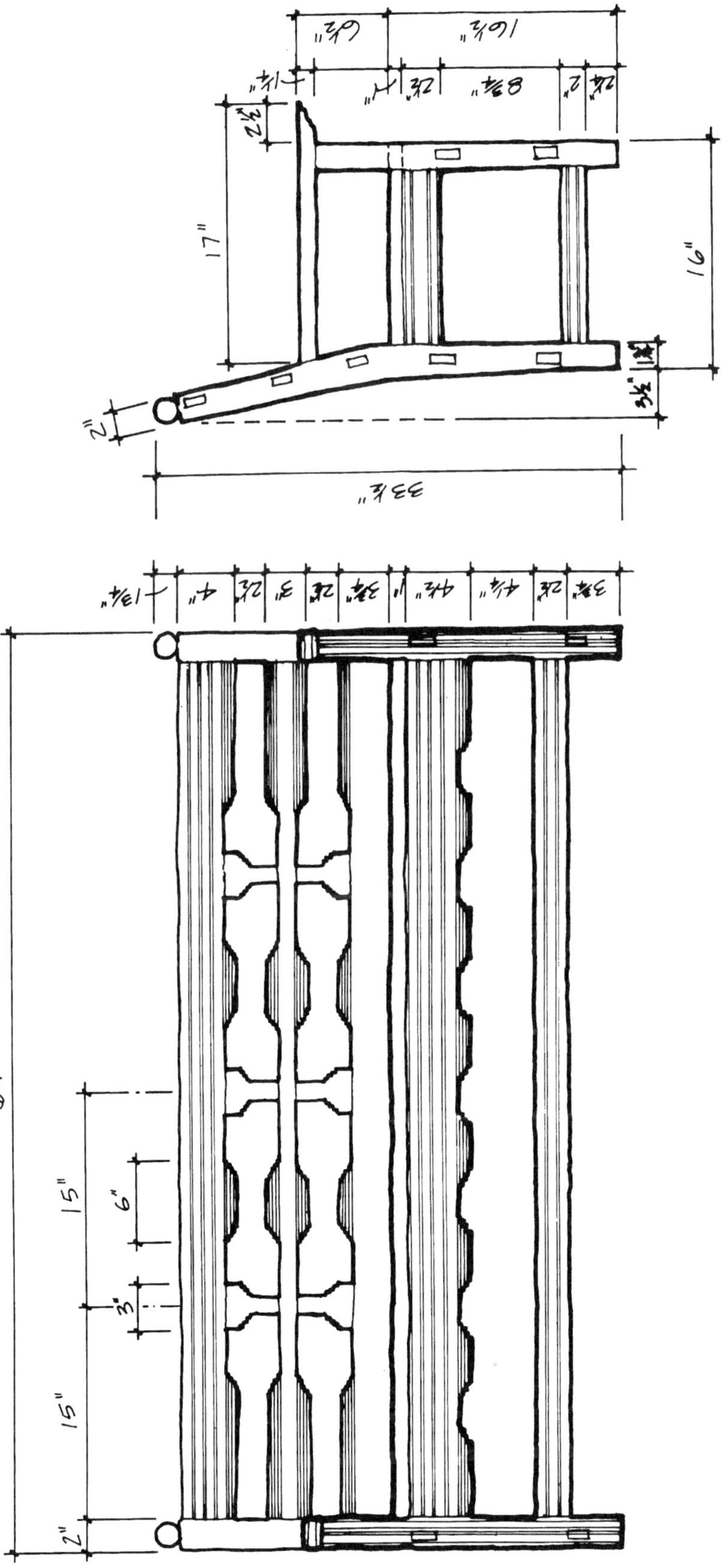

SIDE

FRONT

64"

15"   6"   3"   15"   2"

33½"   17"   16"   2"

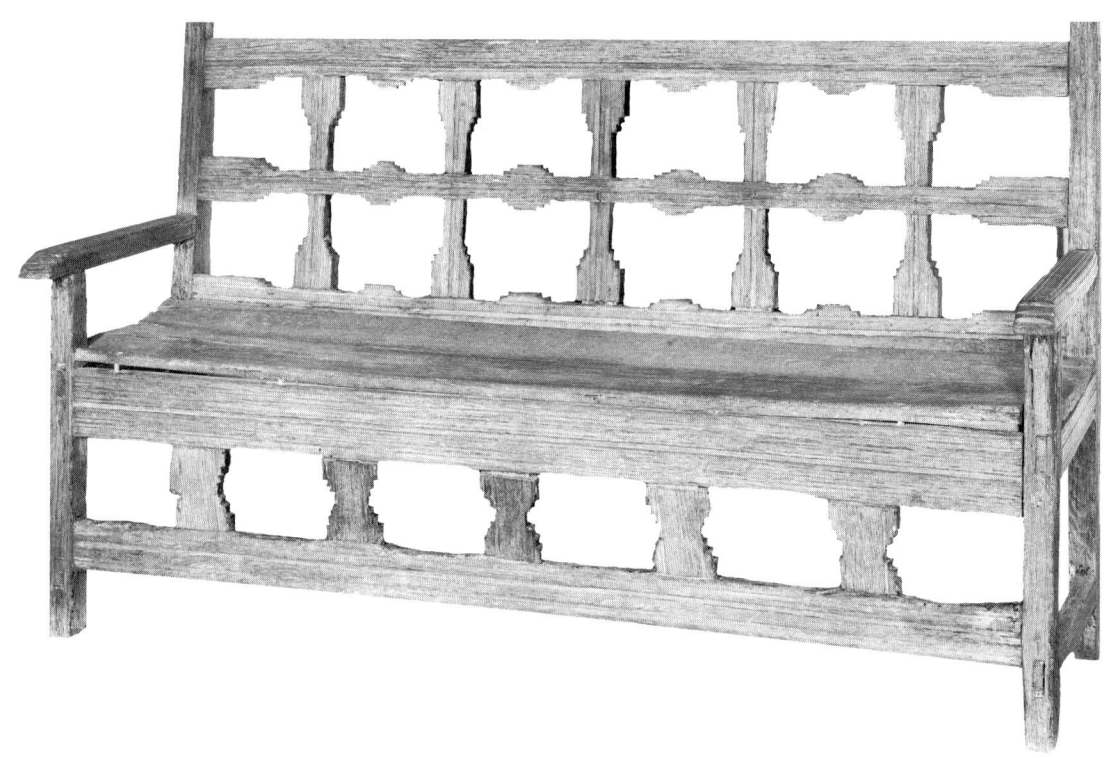

Bench with Five Back Splats

THE SIMILARITY BETWEEN this bench and the previous one (see p. 60) is unmistakable. The major differences are five back splats versus three and the addition of step motif splats between the seat and bottom rails. Note that the arms are carved with steps facing up on this bench while those on the earlier bench are carved facing down. *Gift of the Historical Society of New Mexico to the Museum of New Mexico, Museum of International Folk Art, Santa Fe, New Mexico (FW-117).*

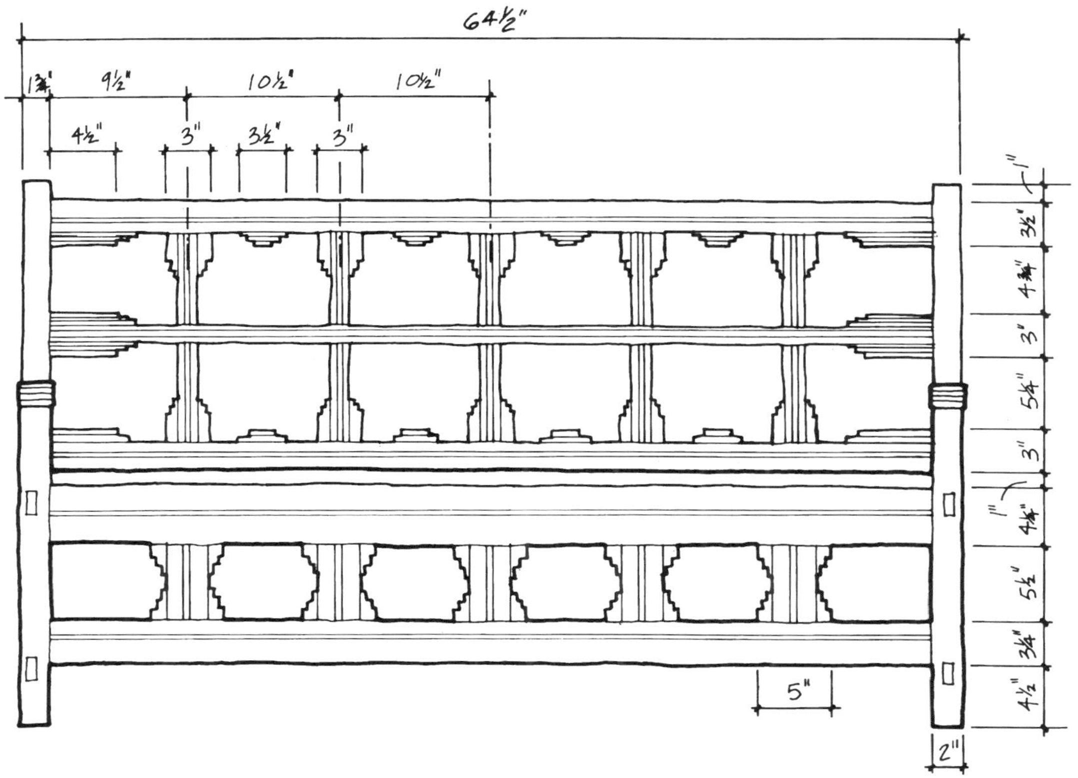

SIDE

FRONT

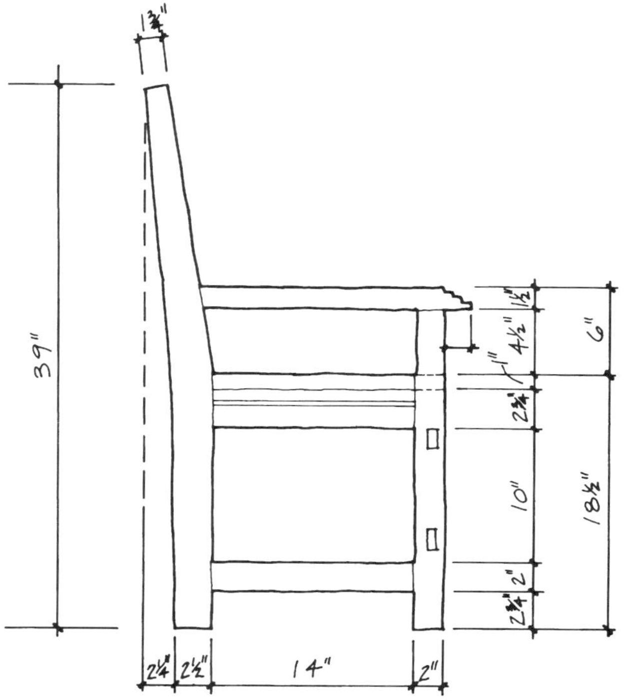

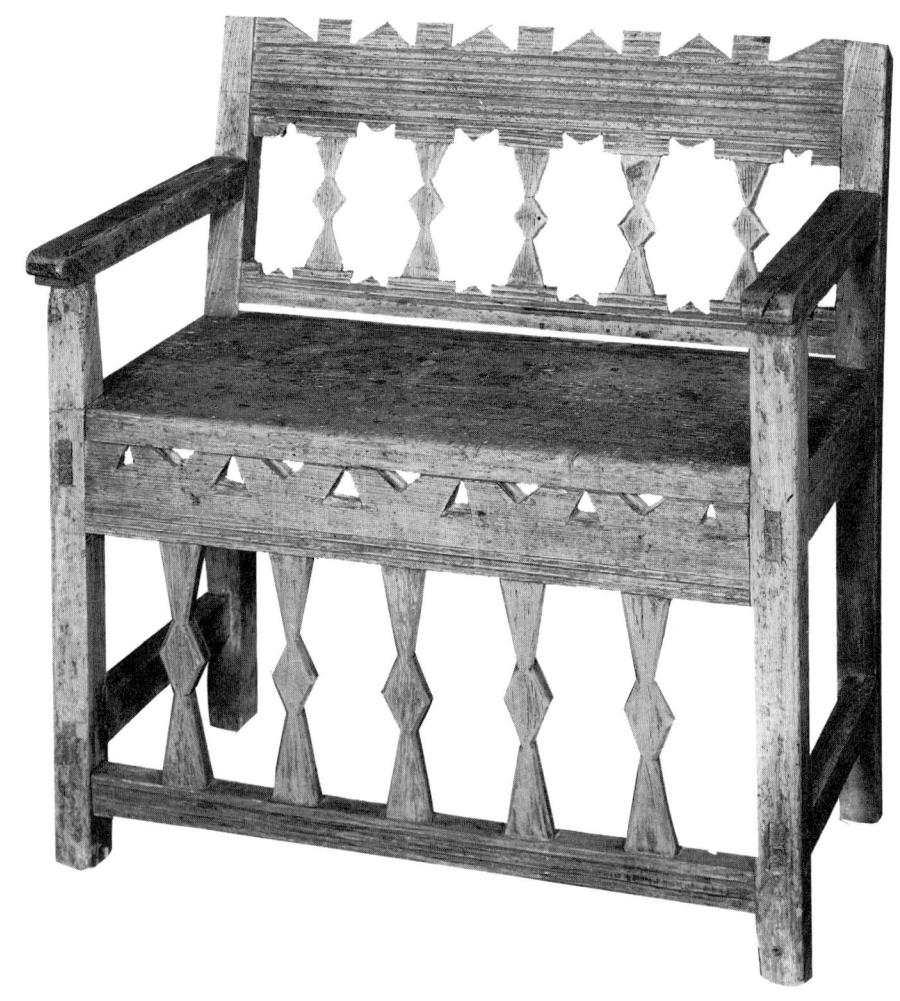

Nineteenth-Century Love Seat

THE TOP EDGE of the back rail on this nineteenth-century love seat is cut with the "M" design facing up while the edges separated by the bowties have the "M" design facing each other. The seat is notched around the legs and a small notch has been cut into the underside of the arms as a finger hold. *Gift of the Historical Society of New Mexico to the Museum of New Mexico, Museum of International Folk Art, Santa Fe, New Mexico (FW-118).*

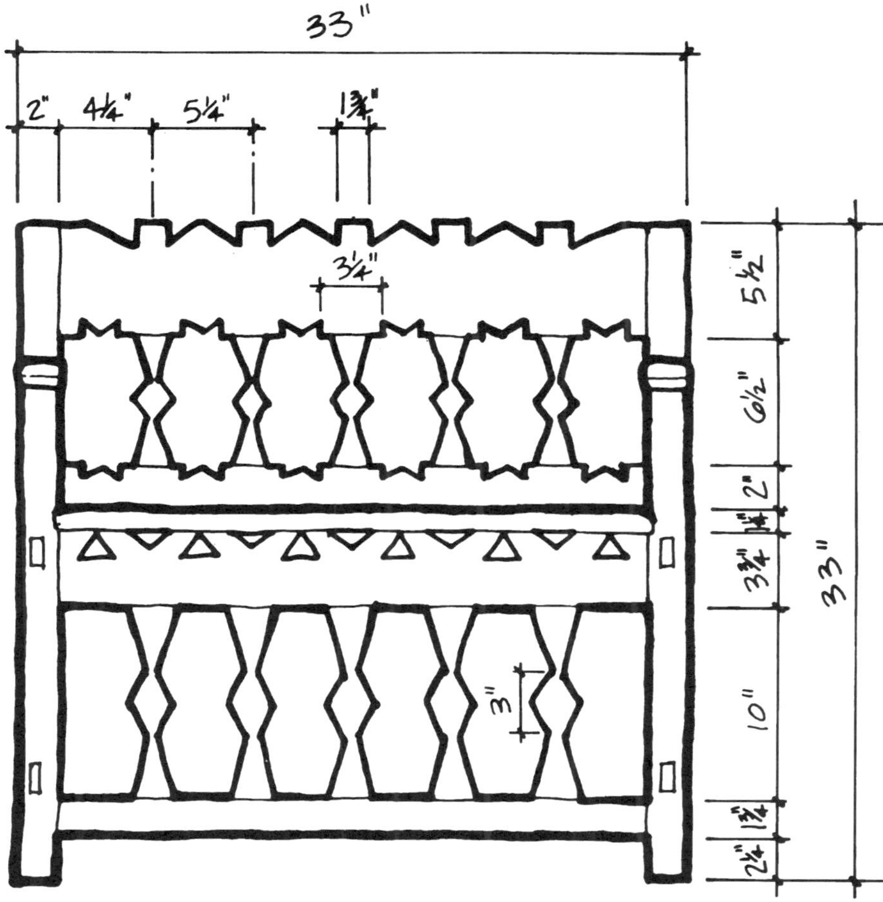

SIDE

7¼"

19"

¾

1½"

2"

2"

4½"

½"

16¾"

16¼"

2"

2¼"

¾"

33"

5½"

2¾"

6½"

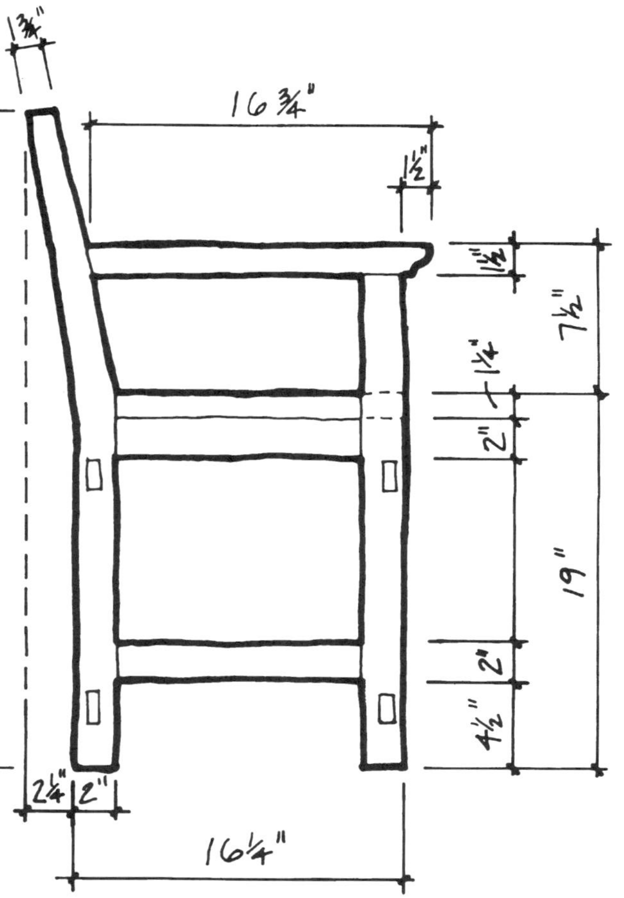

2"

1¾"

3¾"

10"

1½"

2¼"

33"

1¾"

3¼"

5¼"

4½"

2"

3"

FRONT

65

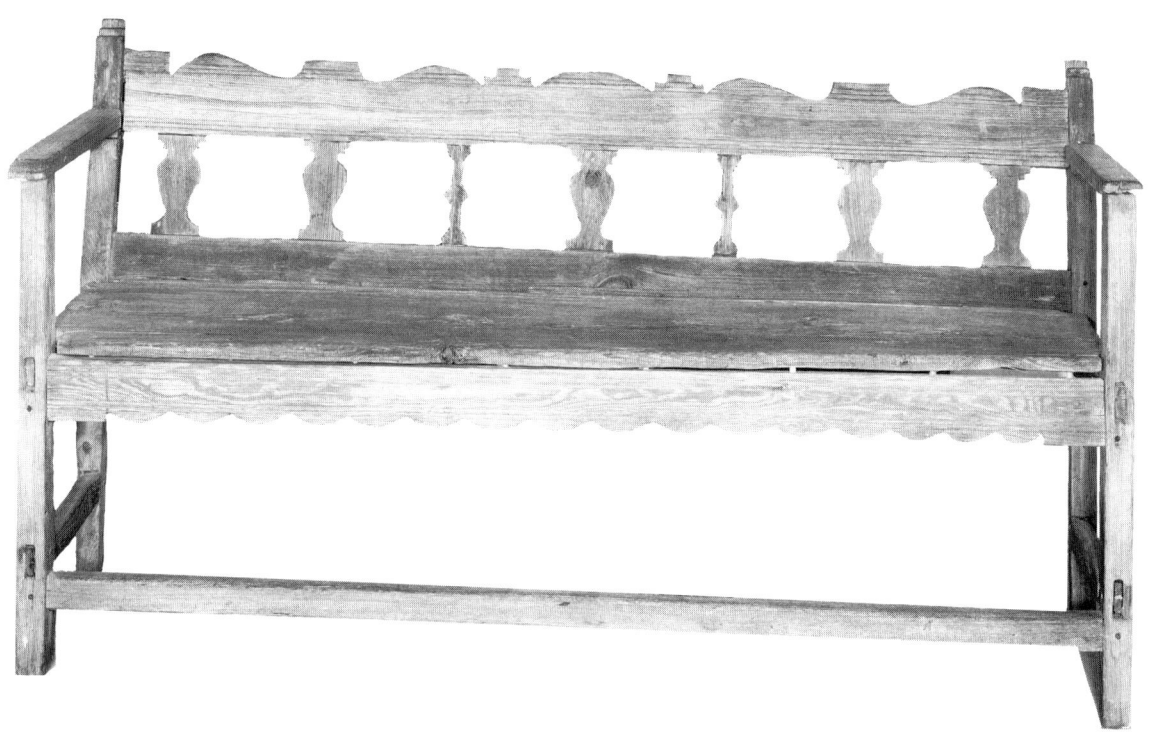

Scallop Rail Bench

THE IMPACT OF Anglo influence and the arrival of the frame saw may be seen in the design of this nine-teenth-century church pew bench with its sweetly curving back rail, scalloped seat rail, and vase-shaped back splats. A single step has been cut into the front of the arms while three steps relieve the top of the back legs. The seat is notched around both the front and back legs. Two beads run the length of the top and bottom edge of the apron and back rail. The bench is held together with overlapping open mortise-and-tenon joints with wooden pegs for added strength. *Spanish Colonial Arts Society, Inc. Collection on loan to the Museum of New Mexico, Museum of International Folk Art, Santa Fe, New Mexico (FW-119).*

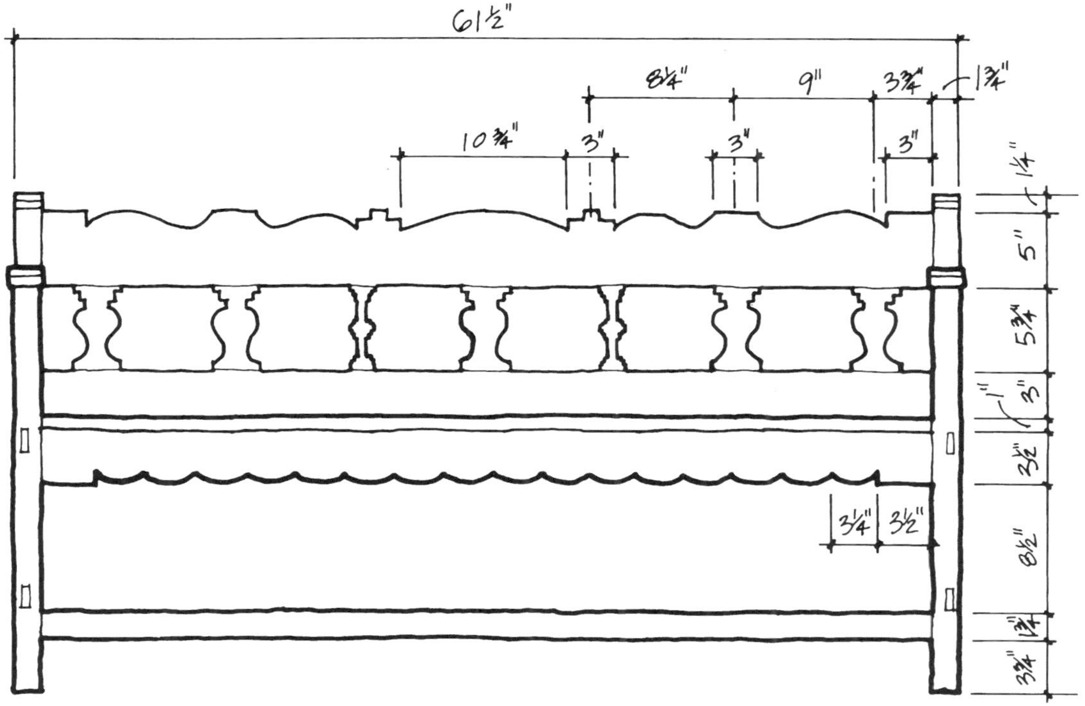

SIDE

FRONT

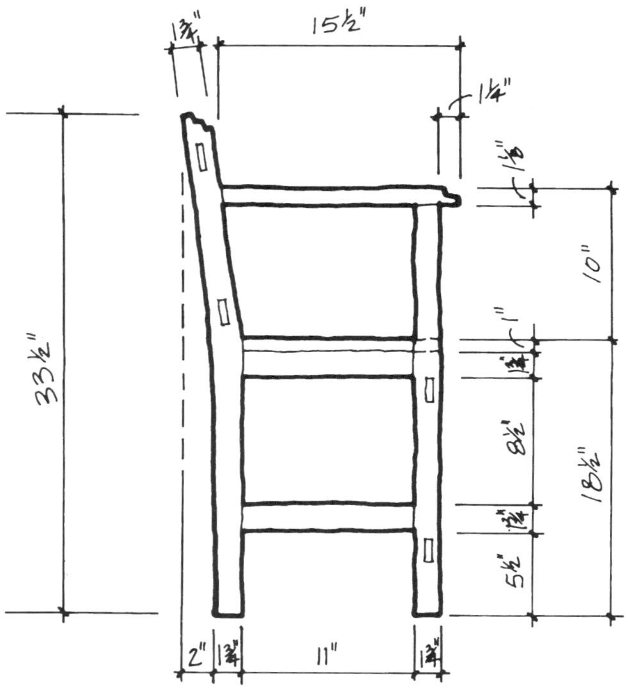

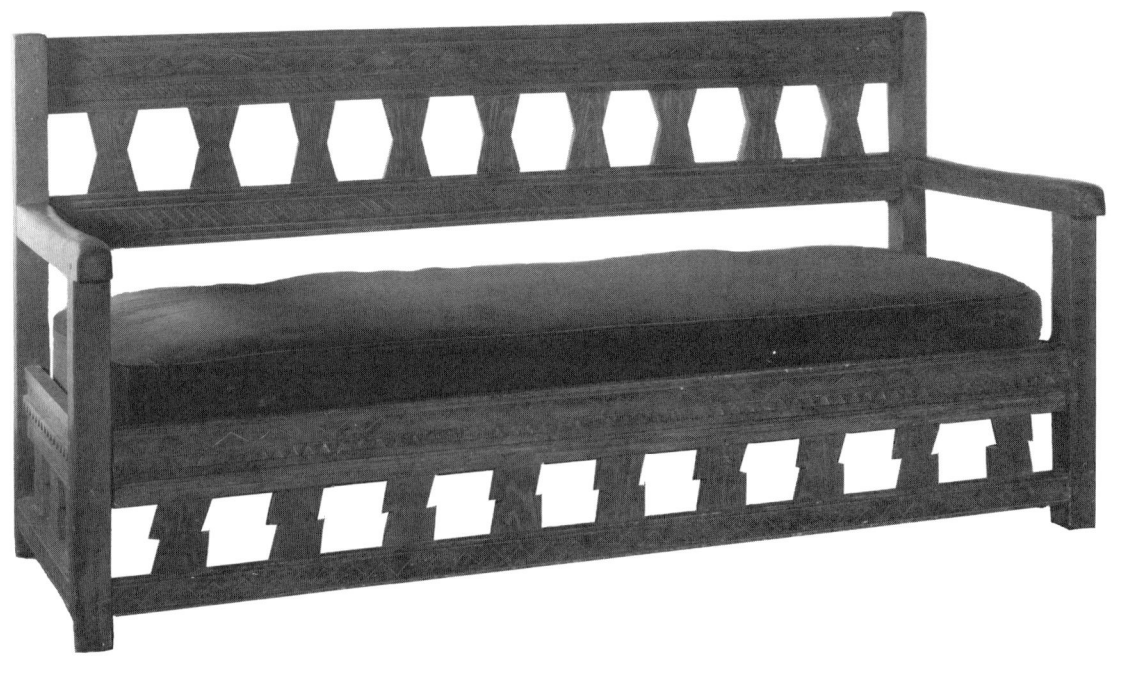

Lightning Bolt Couch

CELEBRATED SANTA FE artist William Penhallow Henderson designed and built this bench, which sits in the Board Room of the School of American Research, many of whose buildings he also designed and built for Amelia and Martha White. With its perfectly straight back it is not the most comfortable bench imaginable, but the recently added upholstered cushions make it somewhat more bearable. One odd note is that the far right lightning bolt between the bottom rails is turned in the opposite direction from the first eight. Three similar lightning bolts were used on the ends of the couch. Plain bowties separate the top back rails, which are incised carved with a sawtooth pattern above and a slanting rain pattern below. The seat rail has the sawtooth carving above a line of serrated edge carving above a line of beads. The incised sawtooth carving is repeated along the length of the bottom front rail, and all the patterns are repeated along the side rails. The tops of the back legs are slightly chamfered and rounded over while the mortise-and-tenon joints are held in place with store-bought dowel pins. The 6-inch-thick seat cushion sits 4 inches above the top of the seat rail and most likely sits on a ledger fastened to the inside face of the seat rail. *Collection of the School of American Research, Santa Fe, New Mexico (FW-120).*

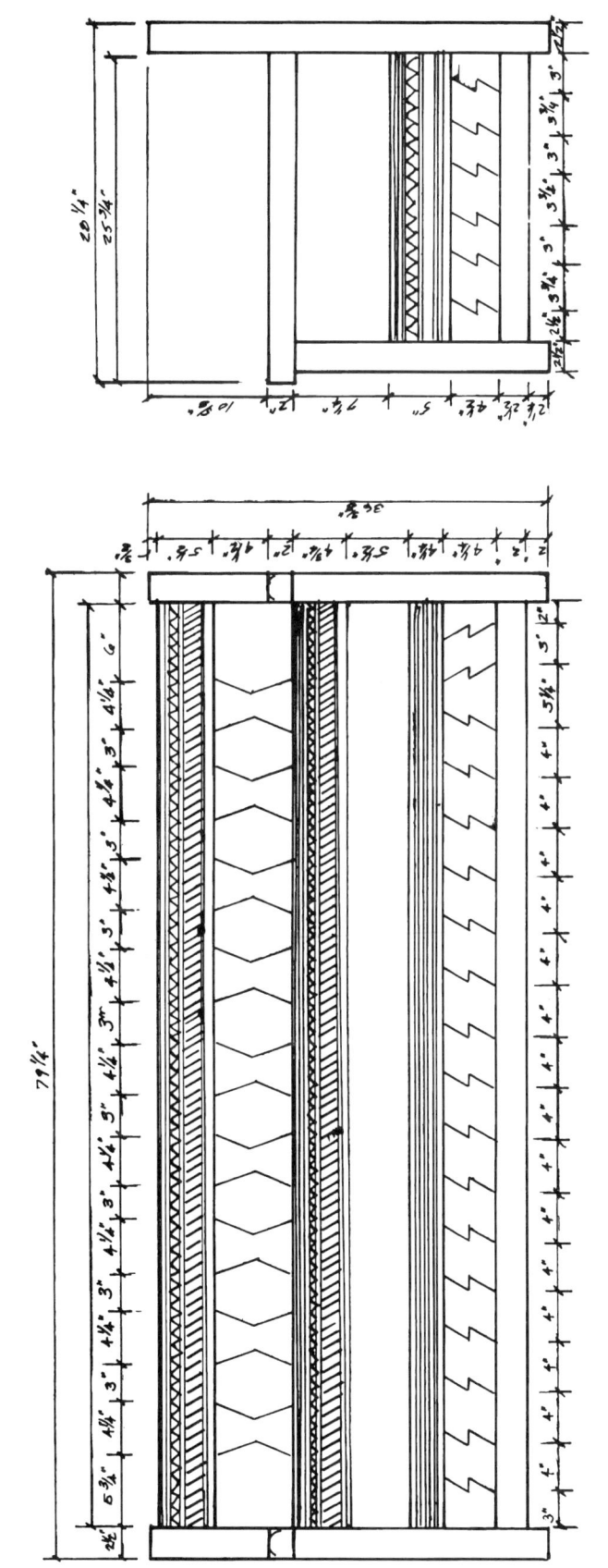

SIDE

FRONT

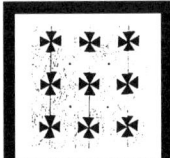

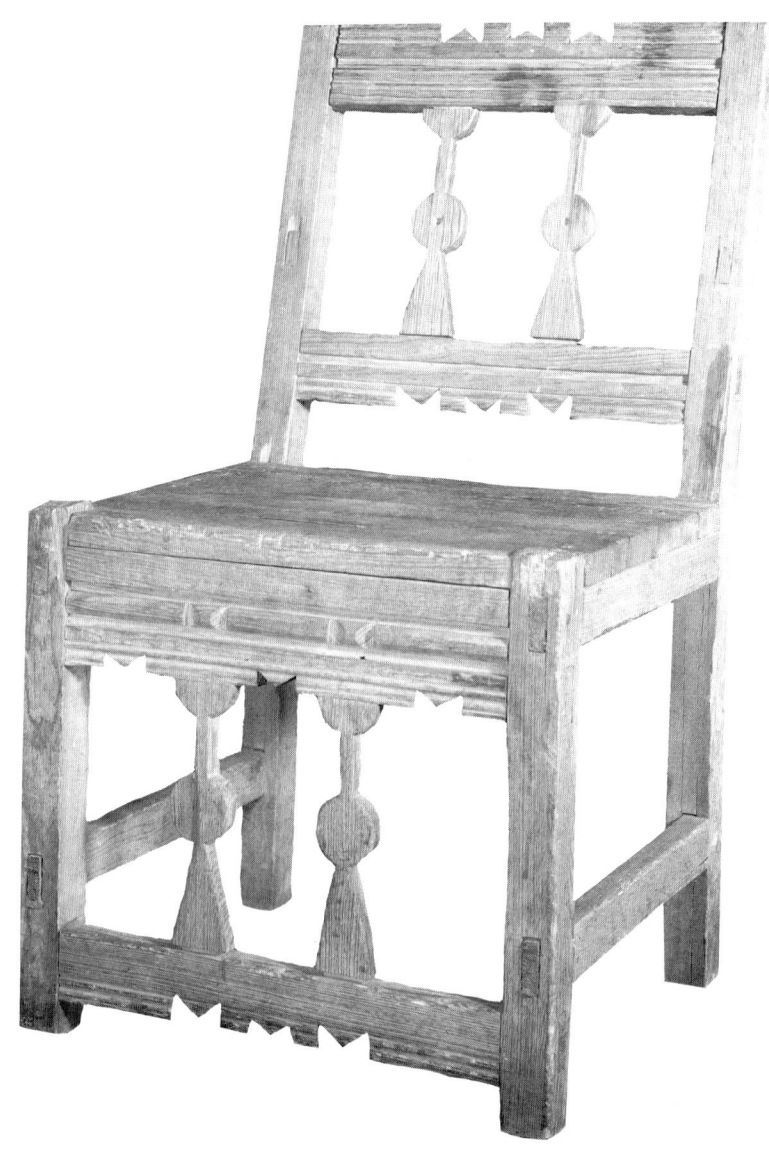

Modified Priest's Chair

STUBBED TENONS VISIBLE on the front of the back legs of this early-nineteenth-century chair indicate it once had arms. Note that the "M" designs face away from each other on the back rails while both face downward in the front seat and bottom rails. *International Folk Art Collections Foundation at the Museum of International Folk Art, Santa Fe, New Mexico (FW-121).*

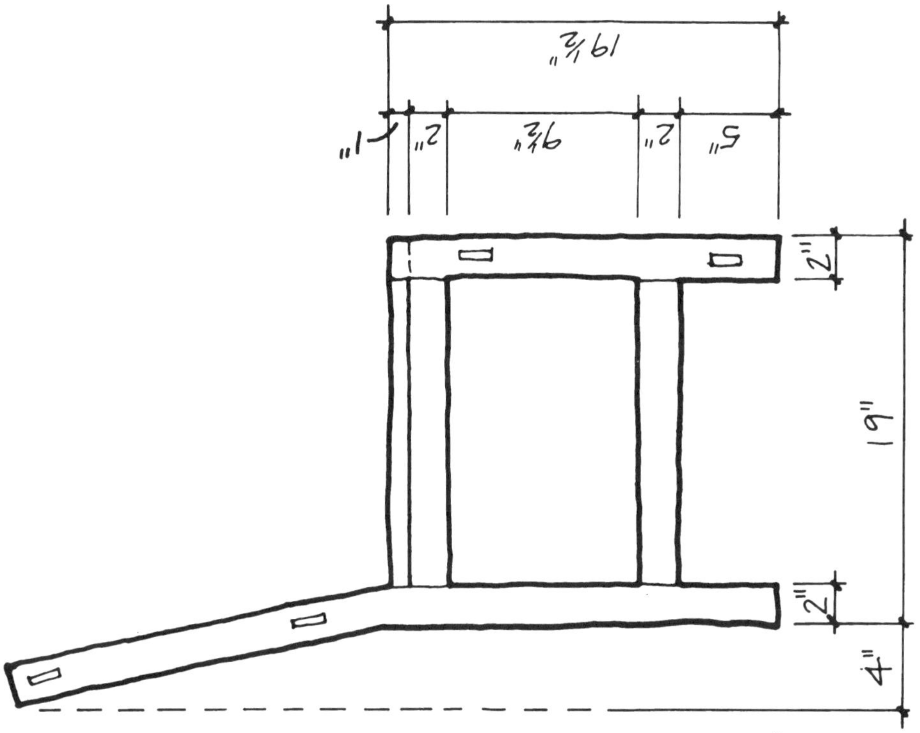

SIDE

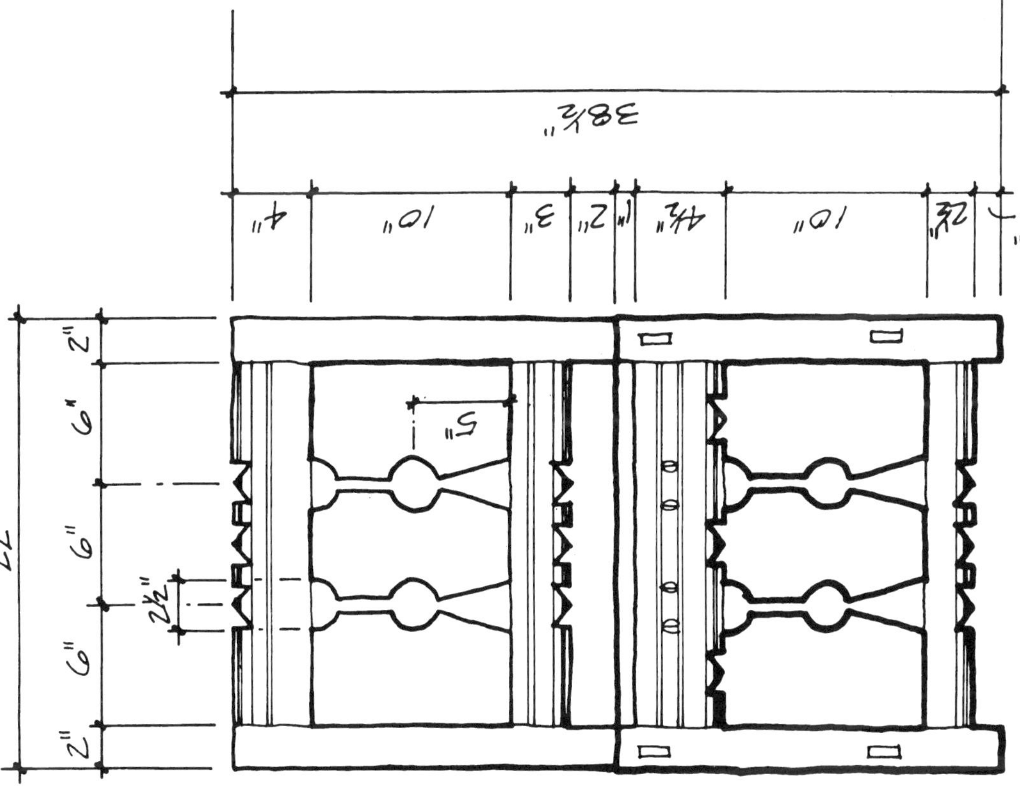

19½"

1" 2" 9½" 2" 5"

2"

19"

2"

4"

FRONT

38½"

4" 10" 3" 2" 1" 4½" 1½" 2½" 10" 3½" 1½"

22"

2" 6" 6" 6" 2"

5"

2½"

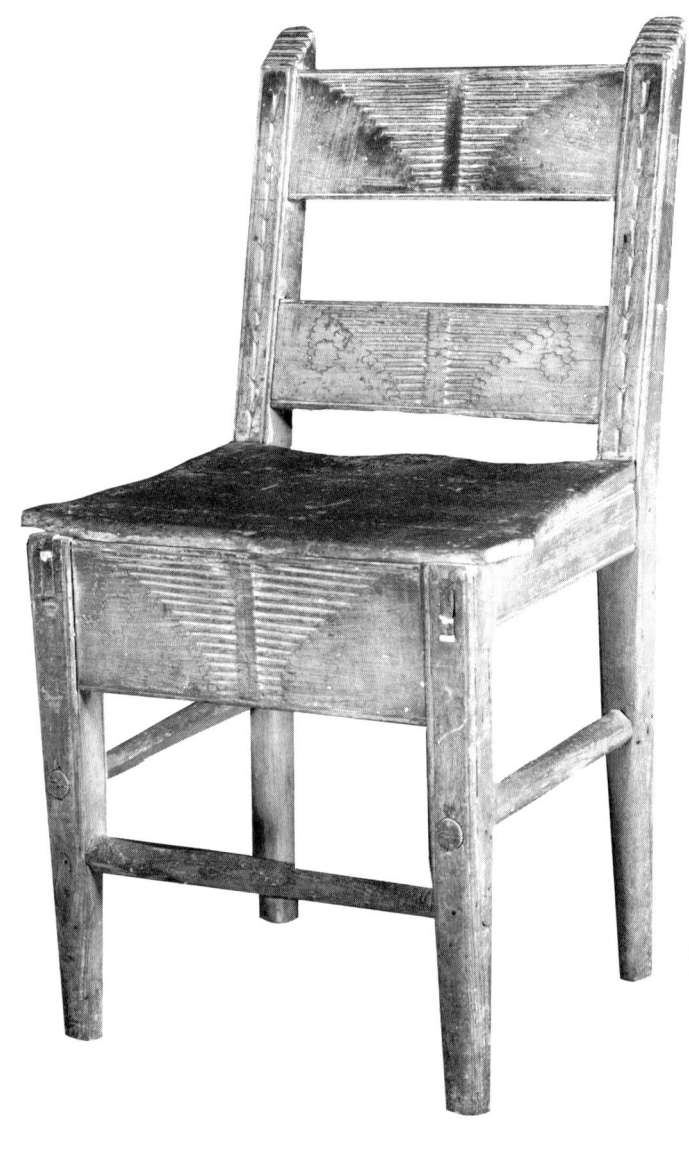

Bead Carved Side Chair

THE HEAVY GOUGE carving along the back rails and front seat rail on this nineteenth-century chair is similar to that found on the aprons of the Carved Round-top Table (see p. 54) and may indicate they both were made at Cochiti Pueblo. The bottom back rail is further embellished with a sweeping pair of ram's horns, while bullets were carved the length of the top half of the back legs which end in a series of small steps. *Gift of the Historical Society of New Mexico to the Museum of New Mexico, Museum of International Folk Art, Santa Fe, New Mexico (FW-122).*

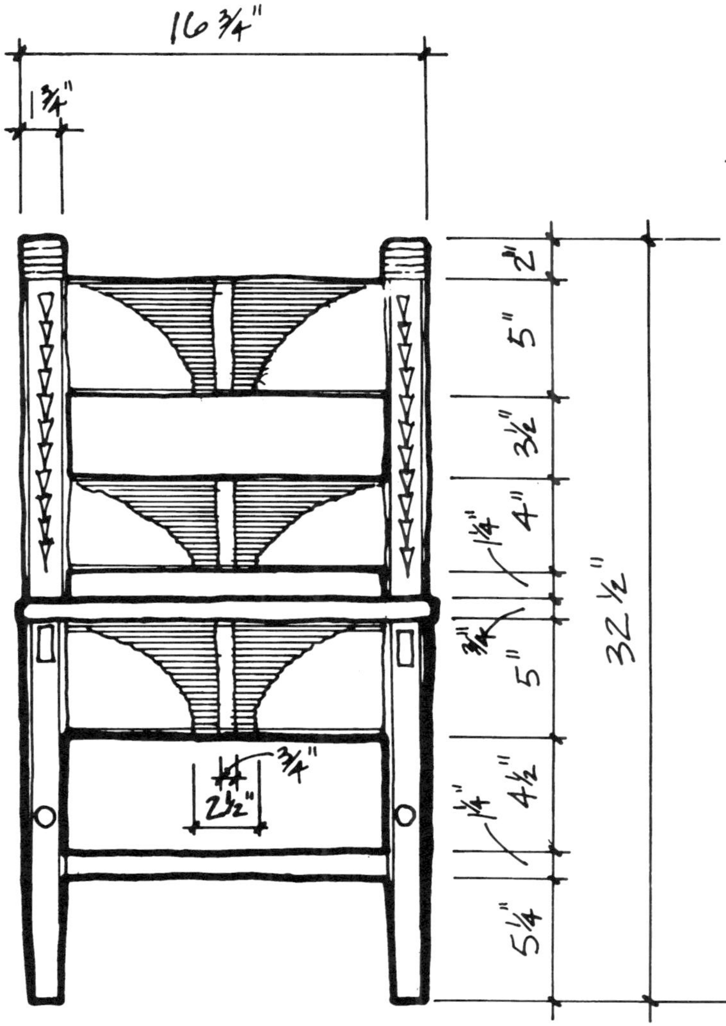

17"

3/4"
2"
5½"
1¼"
7¾"

14½"

1¼"

3¼"

½"

SIDE

32½"

2"
5"
4½"
3½"
1½"
1¼"
5"
4½"
1¼"
5¼"

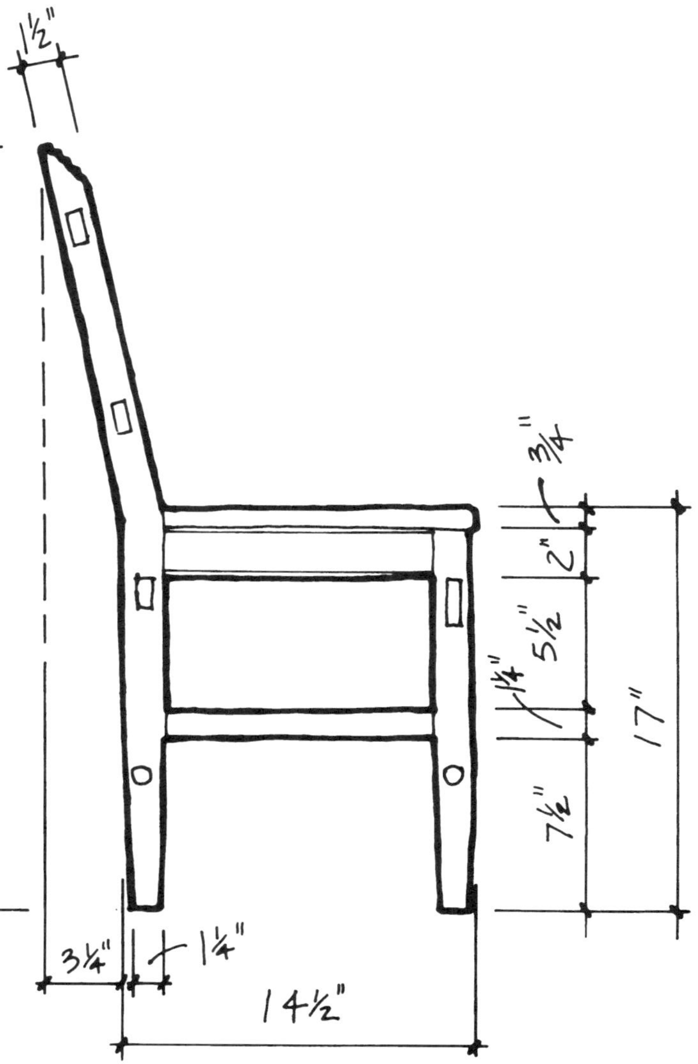

16¾"

¾"
2½"

¾"

1¾"

FRONT

73

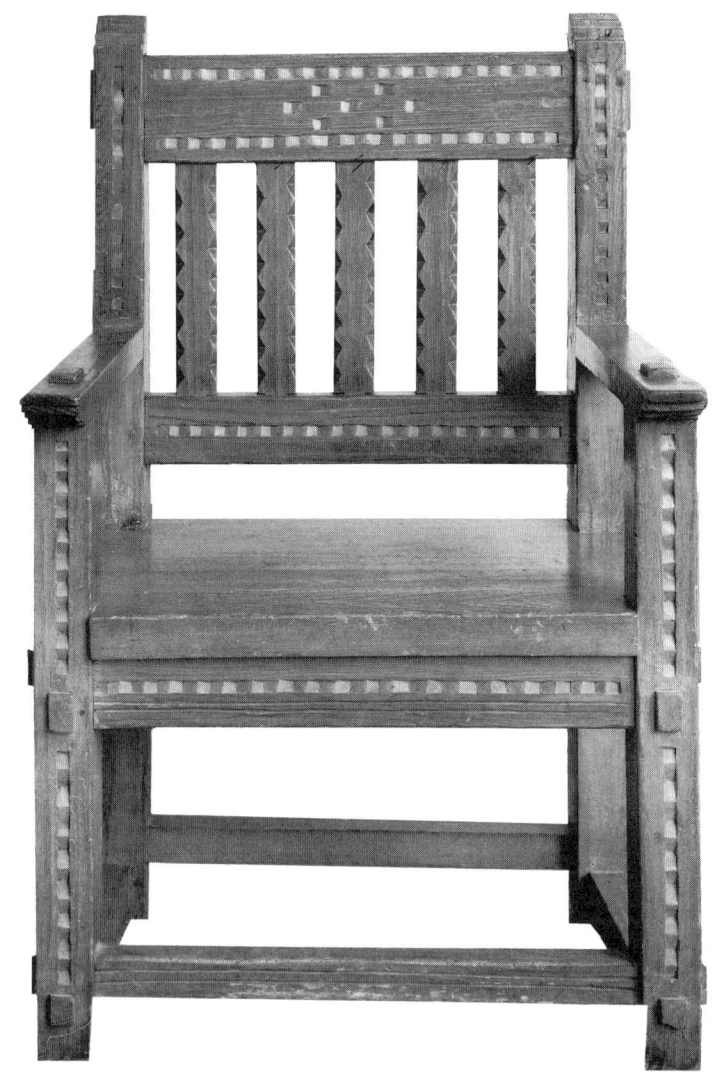

Chip Carved Pueblo Revival/Mission Chair

JESSE NUSSBAUM DESIGNED this chair as part of a collection for the Women's Board Room of the Museum of Fine Arts, which was built in Santa Fe in 1917. The protruding tenons reflect the then popular Mission style while the chip and basket weave carving echoes that found on earlier chests (see p. 30). Two single shallow saw kerfs parallel the line of basket weave carving on the seat rails while the bottom rails simply have the two shallow kerfs. The seat flares out a little bit from back to front. *Museum of New Mexico Collections, Museum of International Folk Art, Santa Fe, New Mexico (FW-123).*

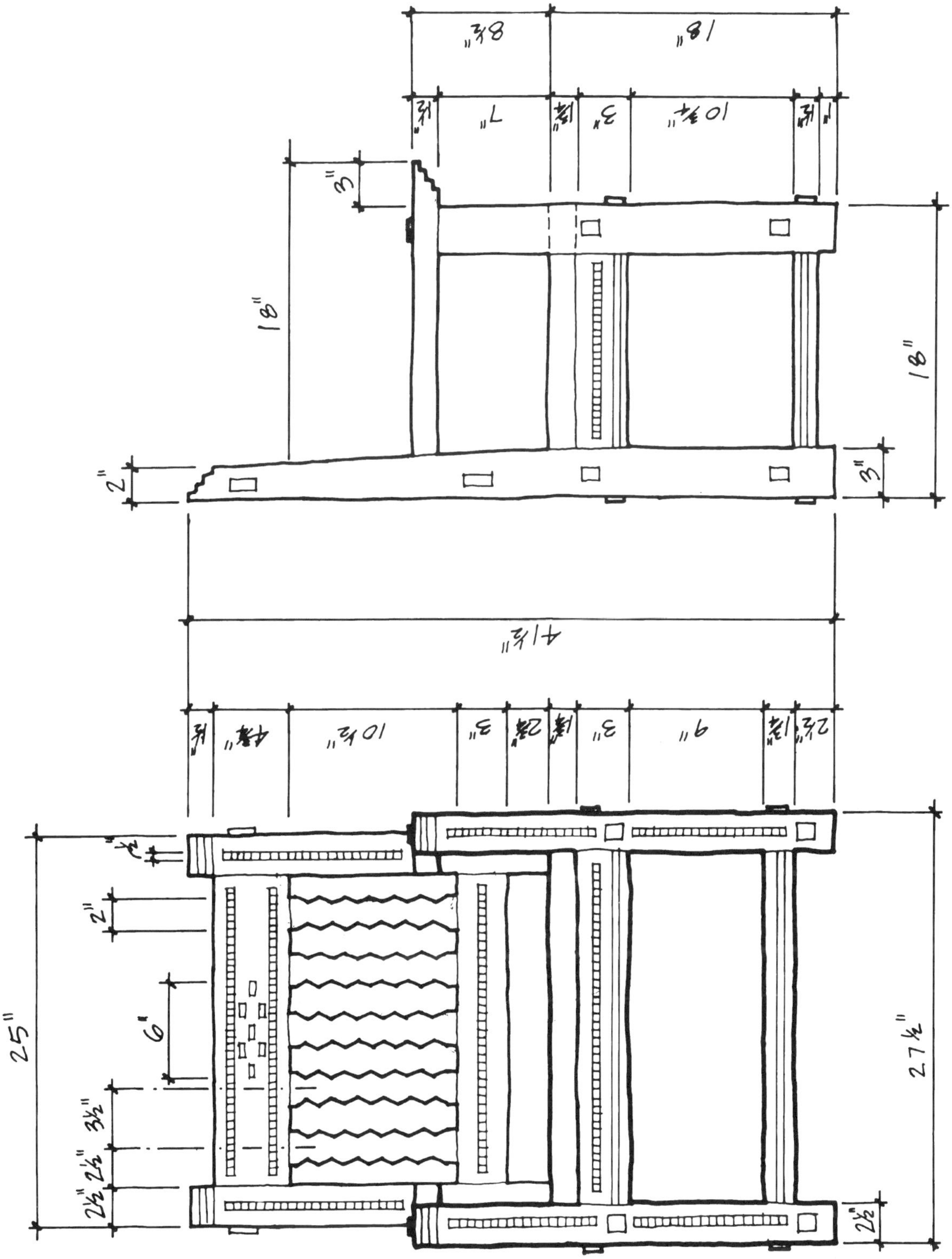

Side

Front

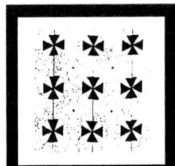

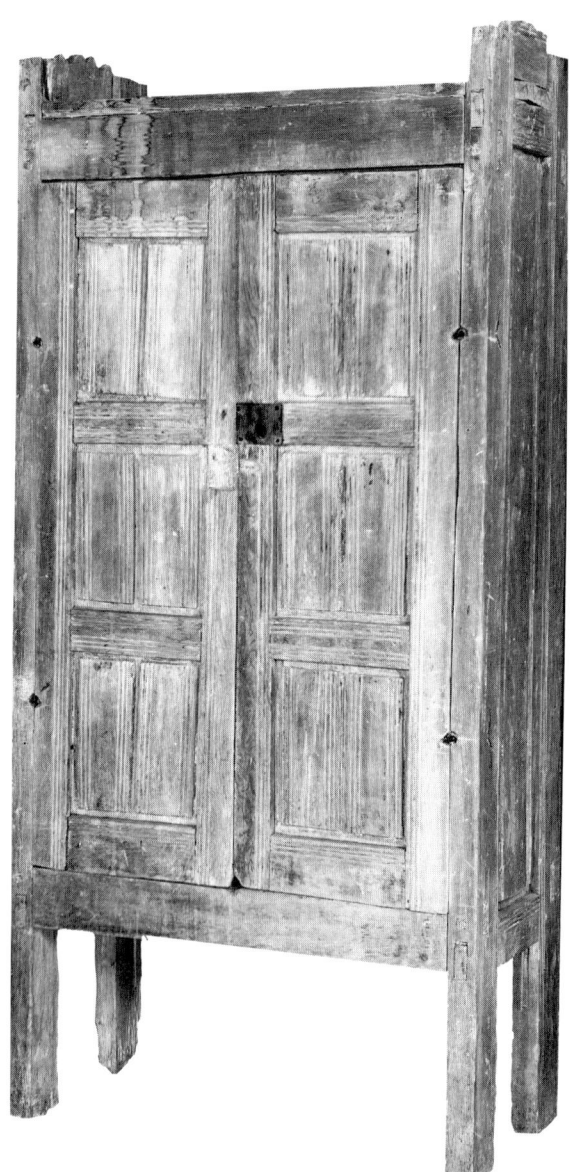

Bead Carved Trastero

THE DOOR RAILS, stiles, and panels of this late-eighteenth-century trastero are decorated with bead carving. The doors swing on pintle hinges while interior shelves are sandwiched between pairs of runners that hold them in place. While the front crest is missing, the two side ones with scalloped edges are intact and slide into dados that run almost the full length of the legs. *Spanish Colonial Arts Society, Inc. Collection on loan to the Museum of New Mexico, Museum of International Folk Art, Santa Fe, New Mexico (FW-124).*

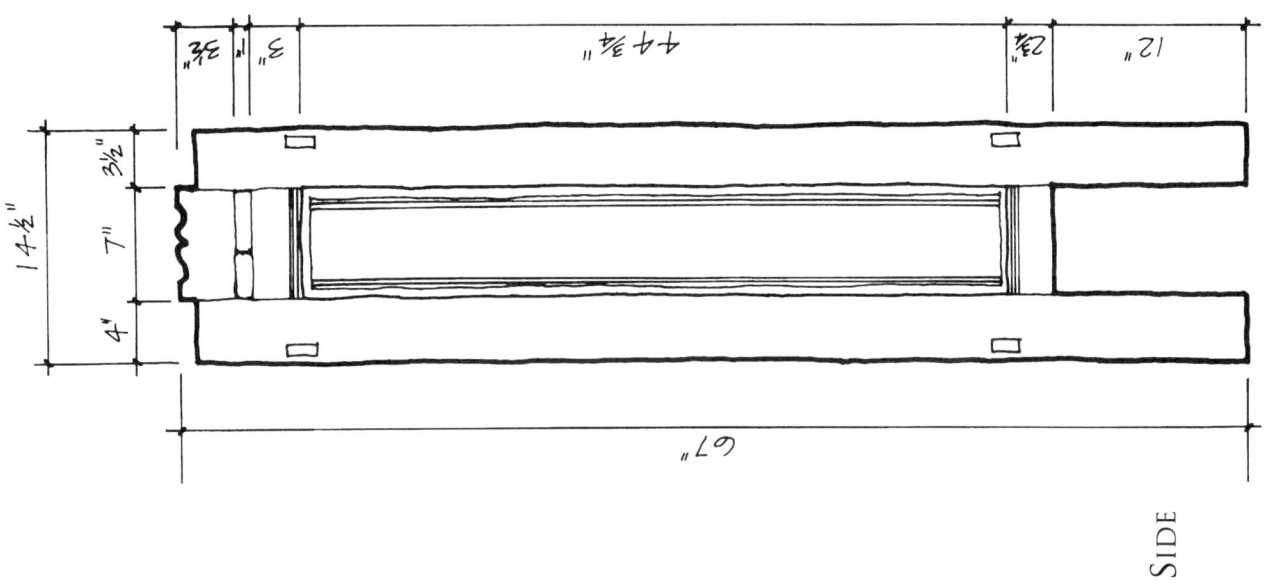

Side

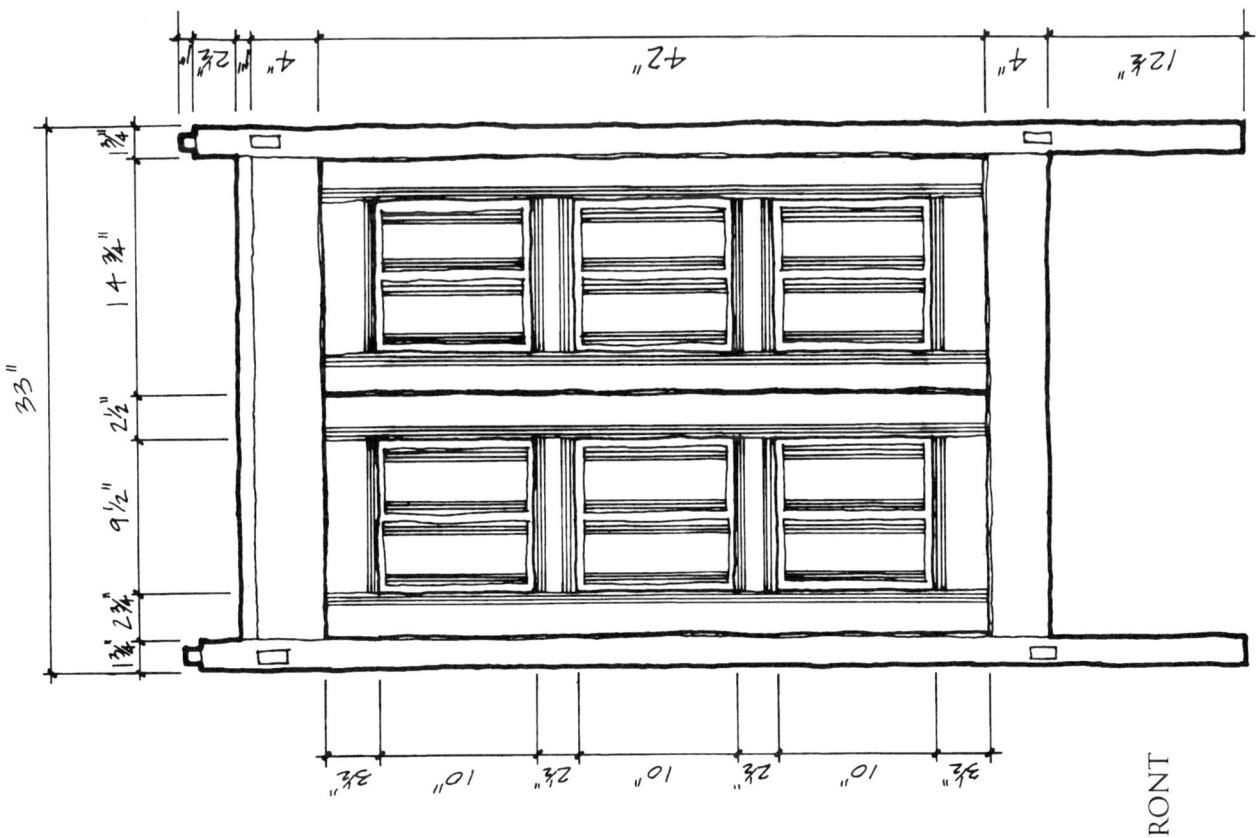

Front

77

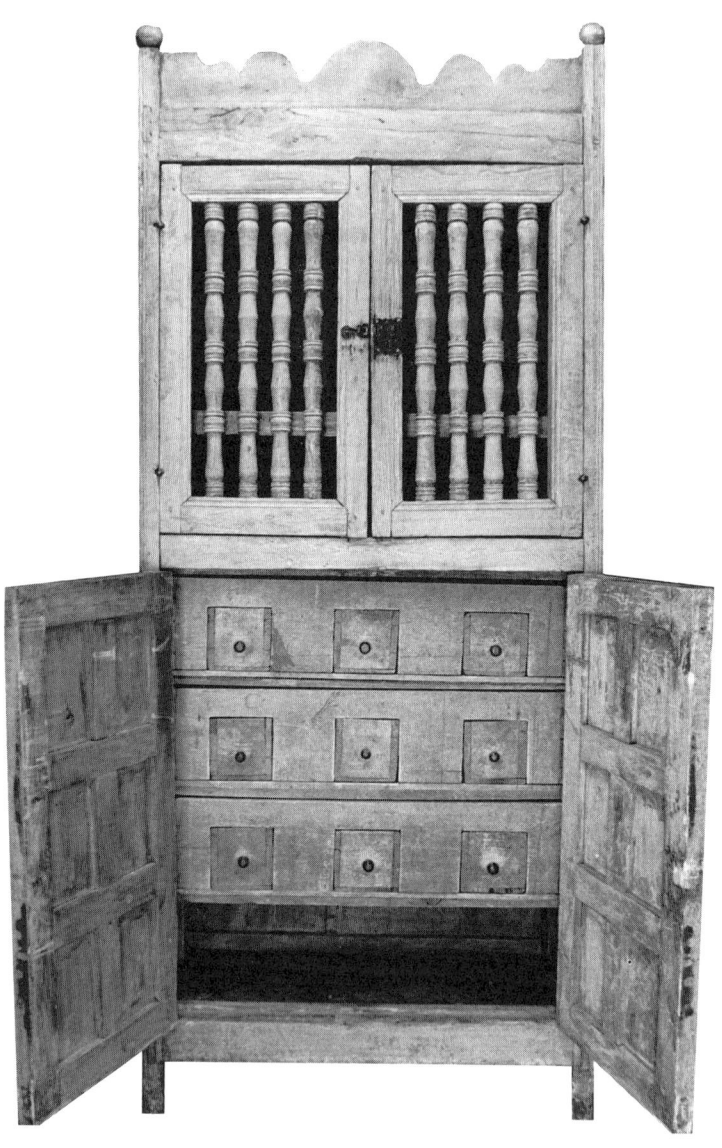

Trastero with Secret Drawers

THE DRAWERS INSIDE the bottom half of this tall trastero offer more than meets the eye. Each bank of three small drawers is set in a box that itself comes out like a drawer. Behind and between each of the three drawers visible at the front are two hidden drawers. This trastero was once clearly painted a strong, deep red as evidenced by the remaining pigment on the edges of the doors, on the inside panels, and all over the drawer fronts. *School of American Research Collections in the Museum of New Mexico, Museum of International Folk Art, Santa Fe, New Mexico. Photo by David Hart (FW-125).*

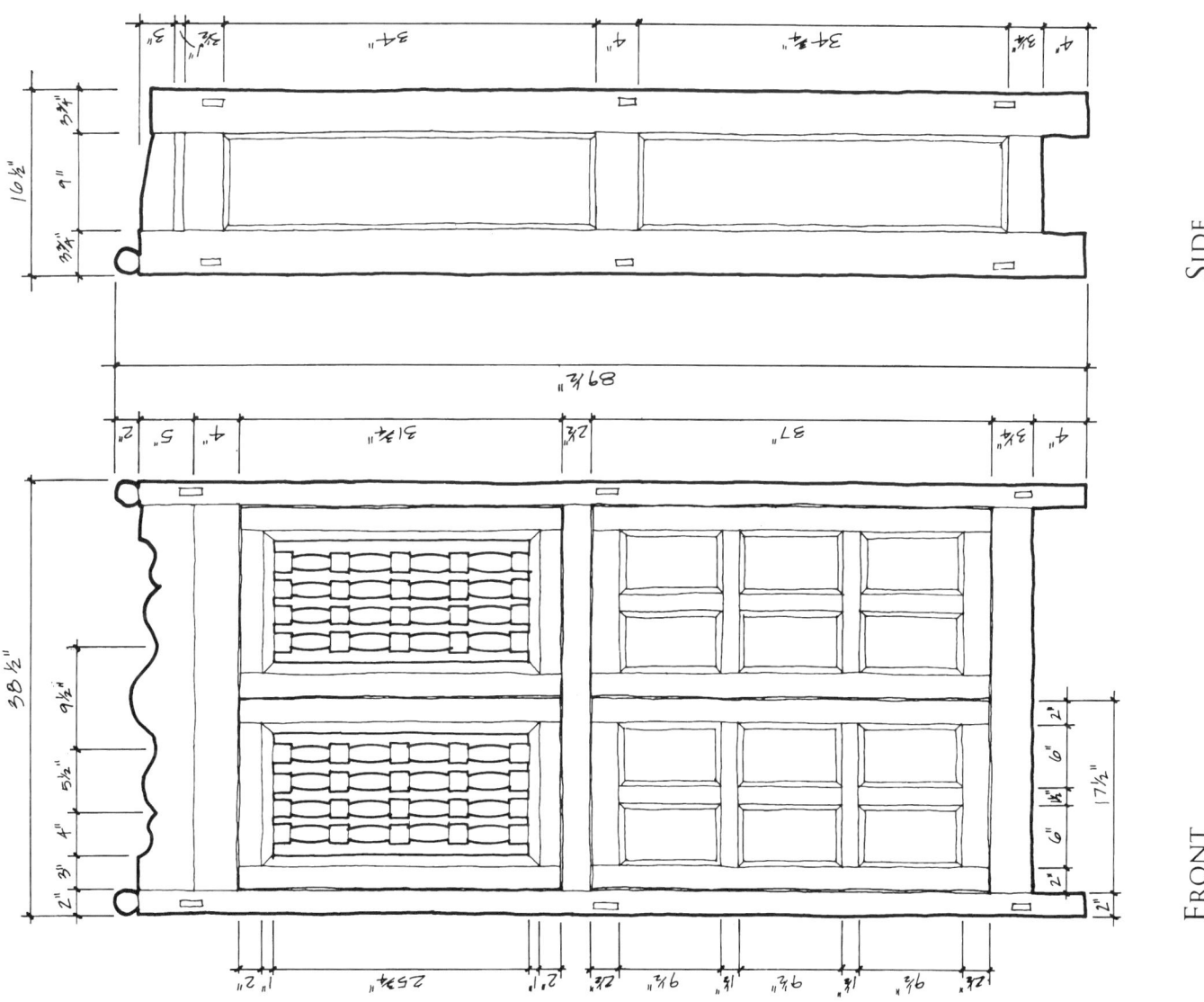

Side

Front

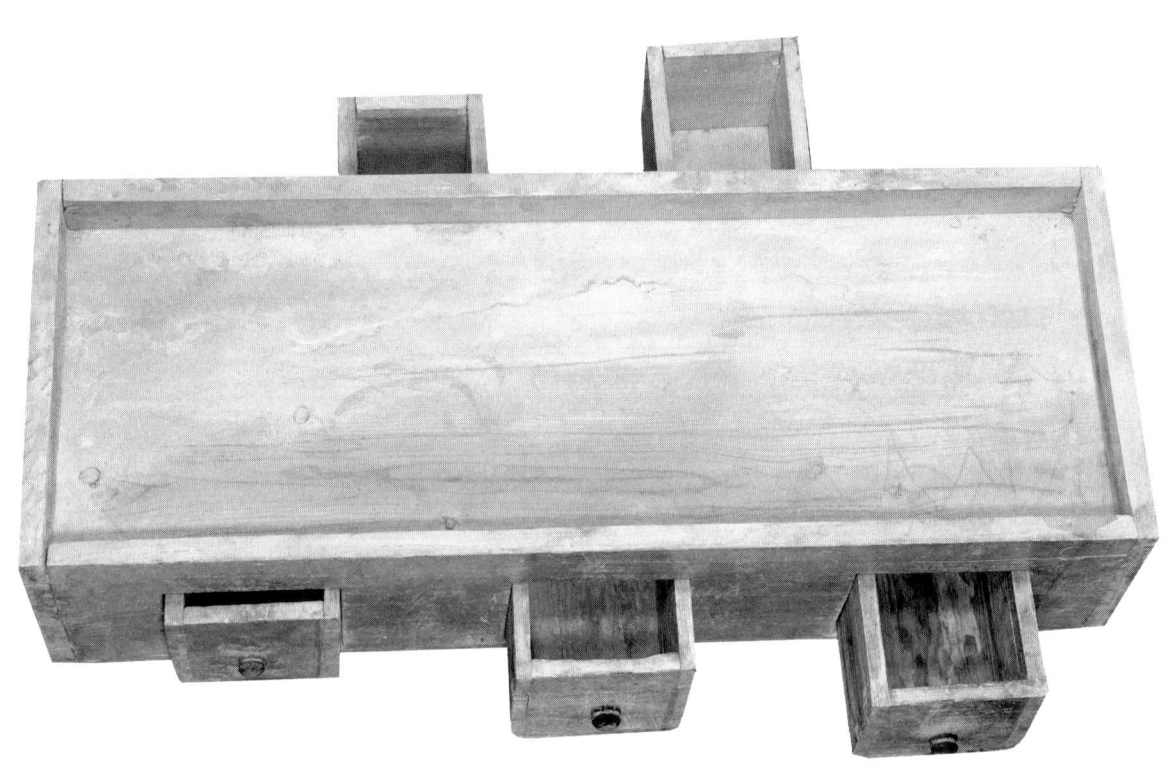

Trastero with Secret Drawers

EACH BANK OF three little drawers has two additional secret drawers. *School of American Research Collections in the Museum of New Mexico, Museum of International Folk Art, Santa Fe, New Mexico (FW-125).*

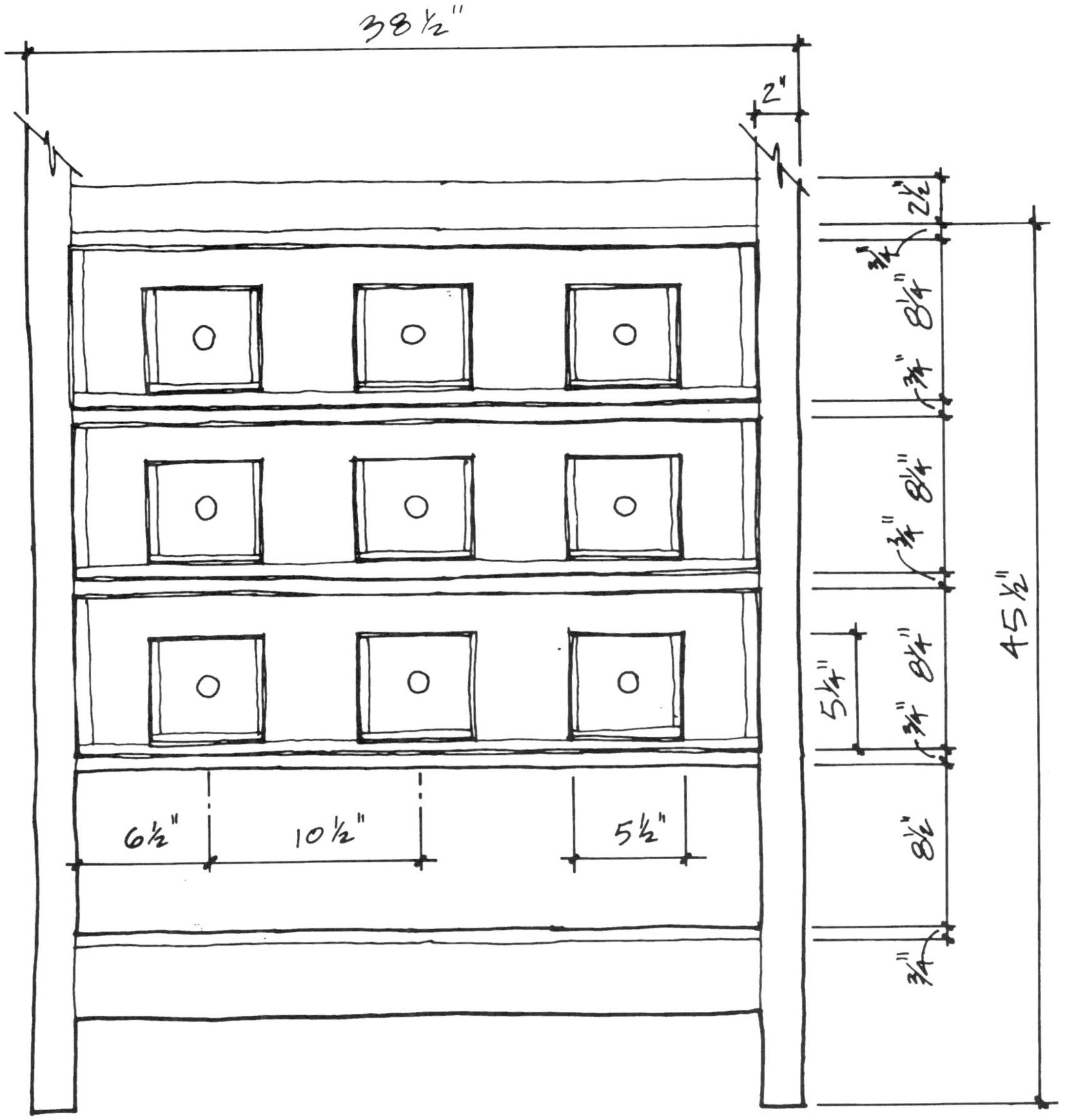

45½"

3½" 1½" 8½" ¾" 8½" ¾" 8½" ¾" 8½ ¾"

5½"

2"

38½"

5½"

10½"

6½"

FRONT INTERIOR

81

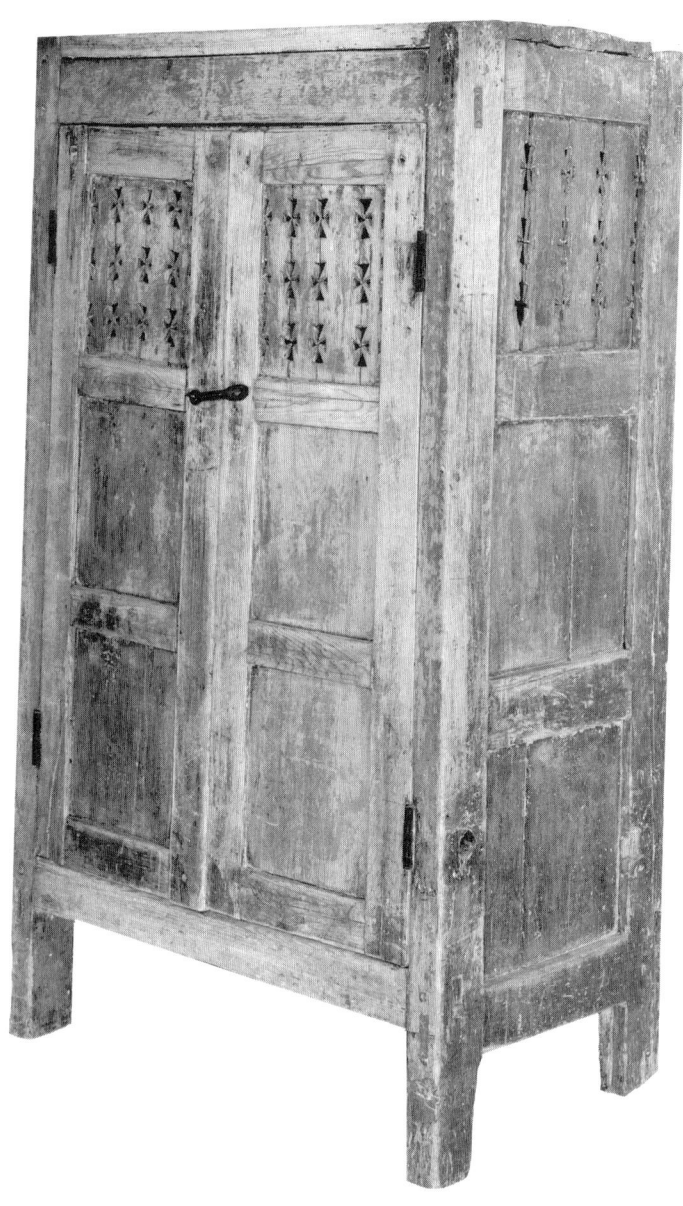

Cruciform Trastero

THIS SMALL TRASTERO has cruciforms cut into the top door and side panels, indicating it may have been either an Anglo-influenced pie safe or used for religious purposes. The top is notched around legs but there is no indication it ever had a crest of any sort. Two shelves rest on the inside lips of the side panel rails. The piece is held together with overlapping mortise-and-tenon joints and was once painted green. *Spanish Colonial Arts Society, Inc. Collection on loan to the Museum of New Mexico, Museum of International Folk Art, Santa Fe, New Mexico (FW-126).*

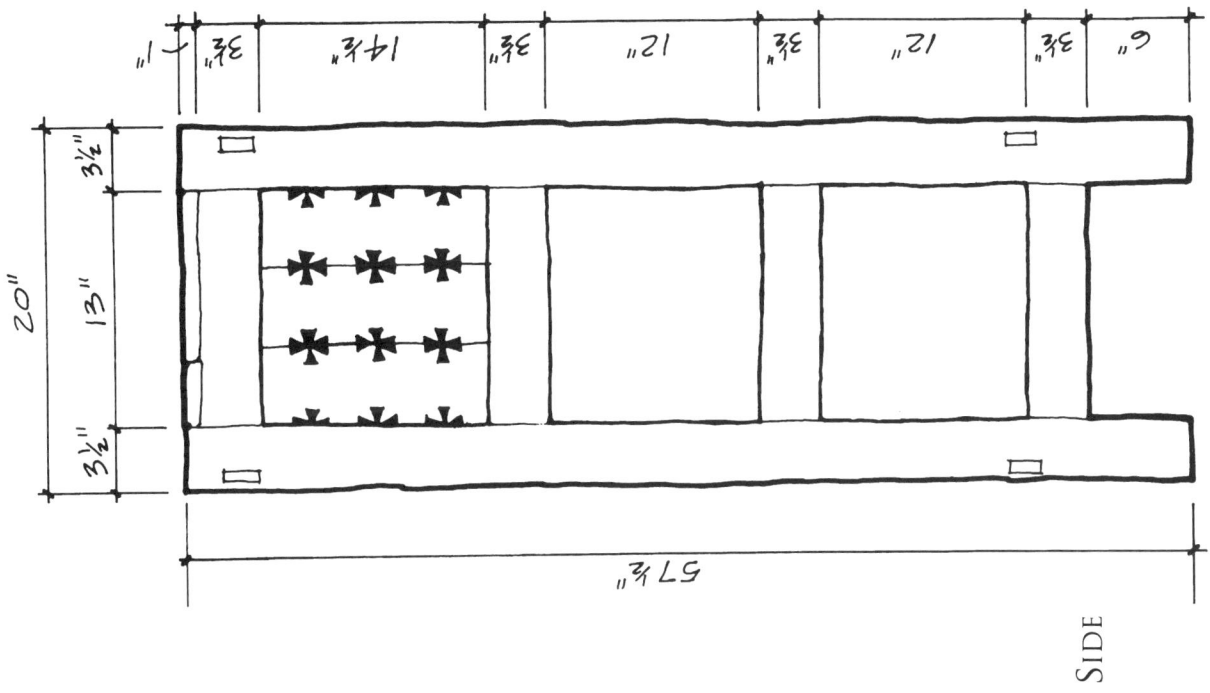

SIDE

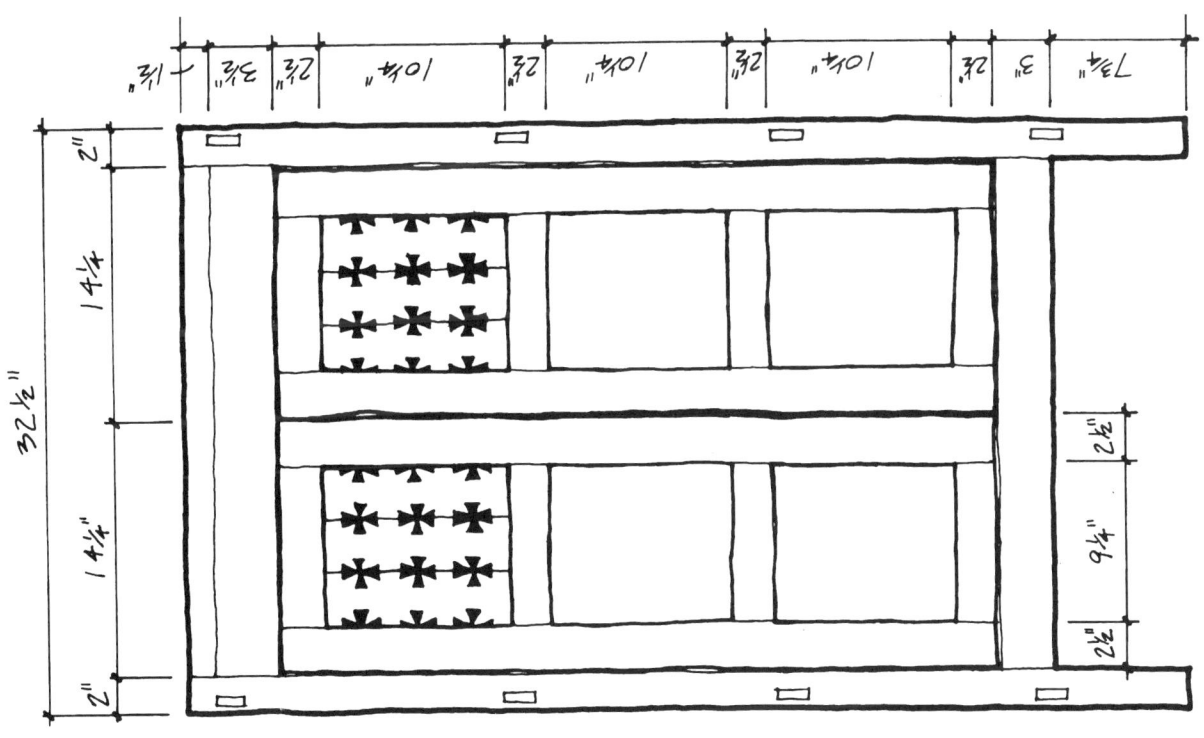

FRONT

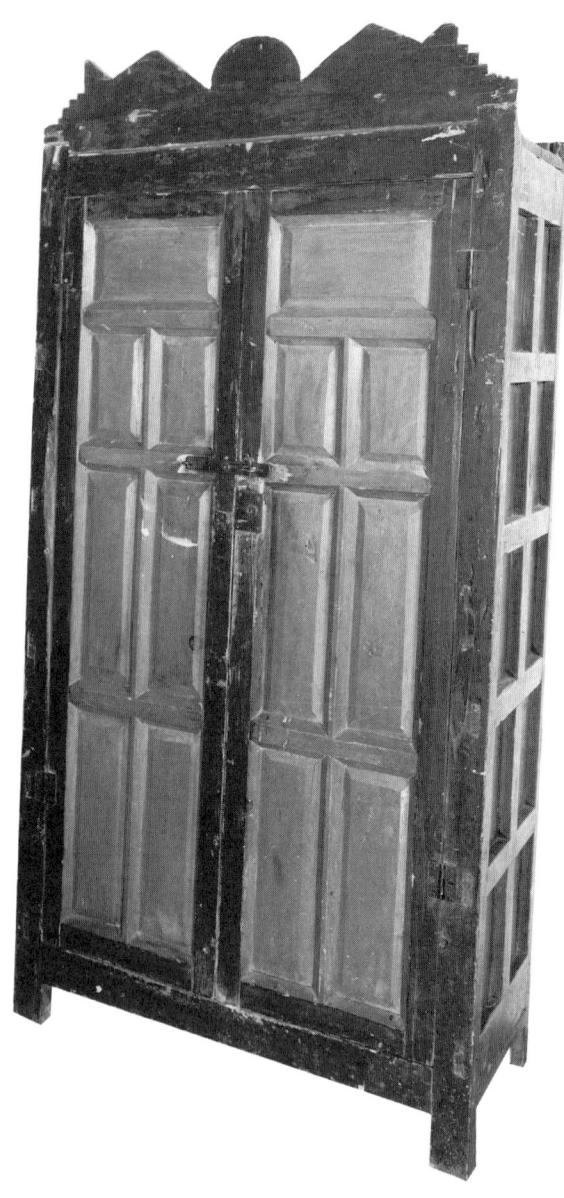

Beveled Panel Trastero

AT ONE TIME this trastero must have been built into a wall or another fixture because the left side is unpainted and shows the saw scars of having been removed from an earlier installation. The raised door panels are painted a bright red while the door and case frames, sides, and crown are a dark brown. The front door panel dividers are deeply chamfered, but the side panels and frames have been left square. *Collection of the School of American Research, Santa Fe, New Mexico (FW-127).*

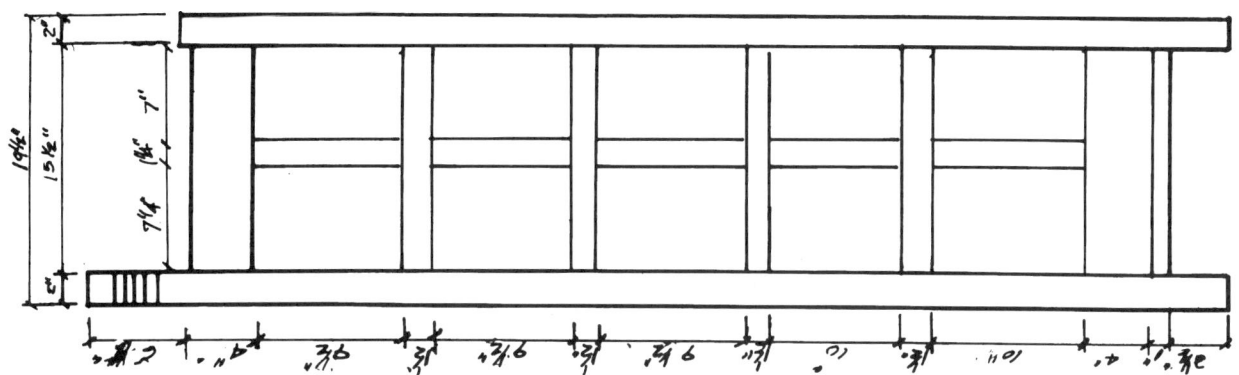

SIDE

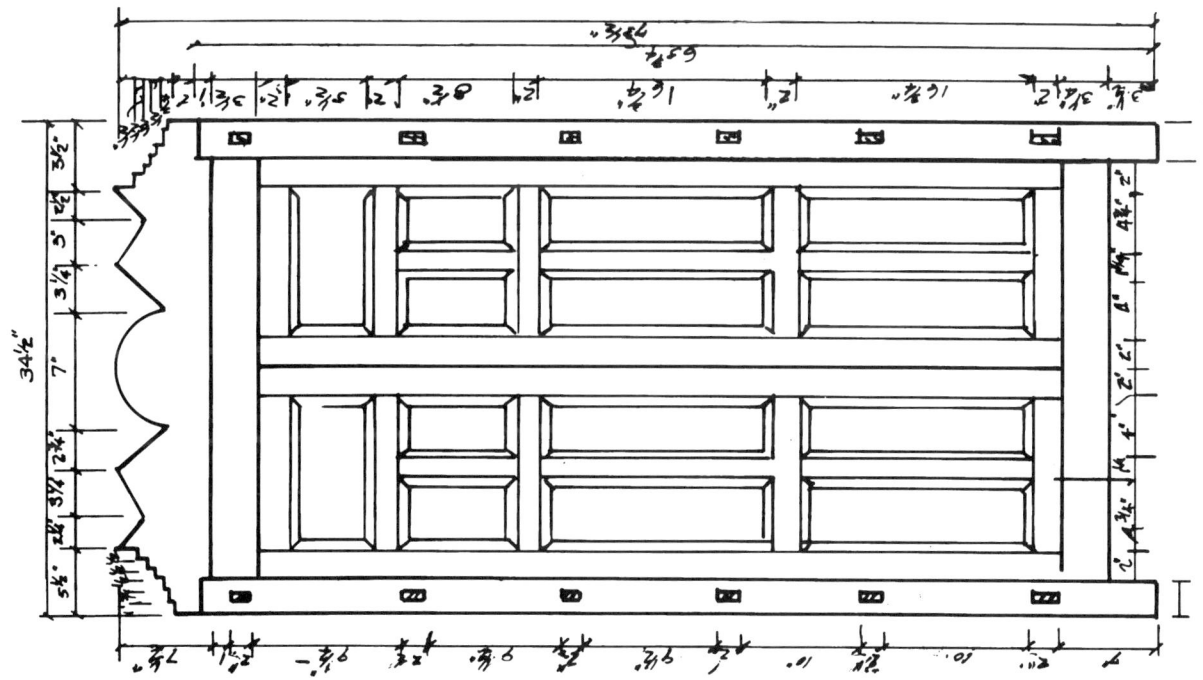

FRONT

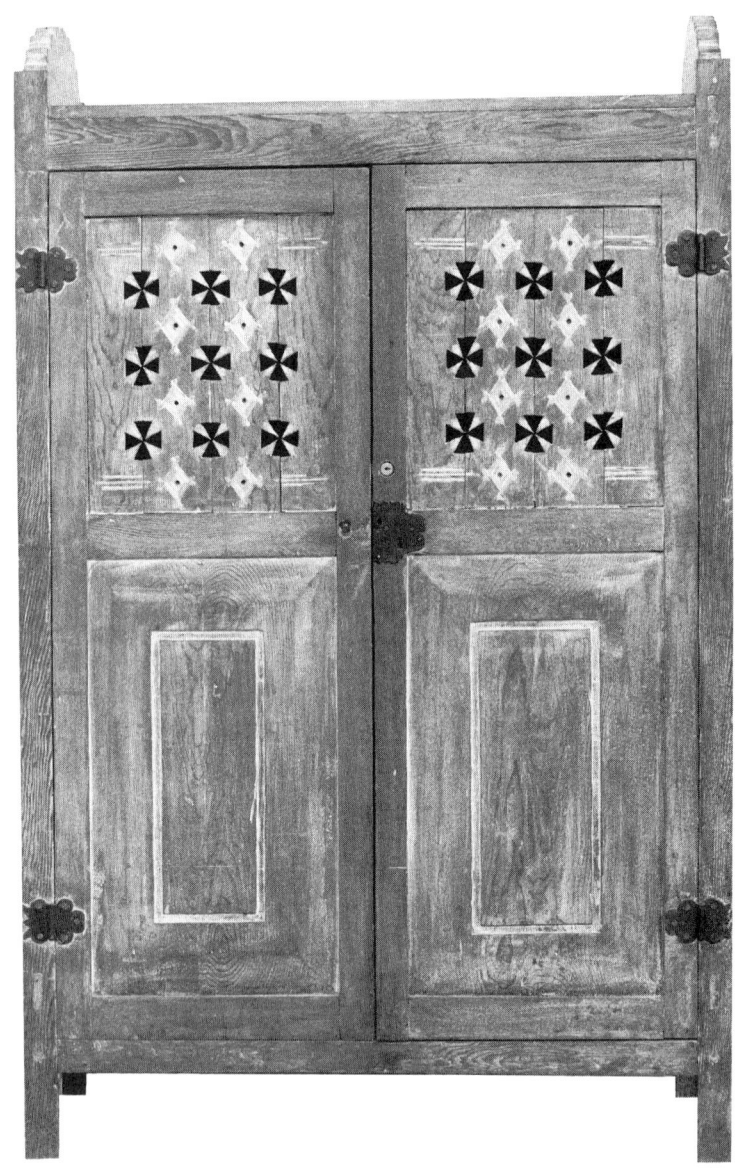

Crested Trastero

IT IS BELIEVED that this trastero was built in 1935 in Roswell, New Mexico, by Domingo Tejada, the main carpenter in charge of furniture building for Works Progress Administration's construction of the Roswell Museum and Art Center. The cruciforms cut into the doors echo those on the much earlier Cruciform Trastero (see p. 82). The "God's eyes" that sit between the cutouts are made from straw glued to the surface of the cabinet. The two side crests slide in grooves cut into the legs that extend above the top side rail. *Permanent Collection, Roswell Museum and Art Center, Gift of Federal Art Project, WPA 1994.18.17. Photo by Jose Rivera (FW-128).*

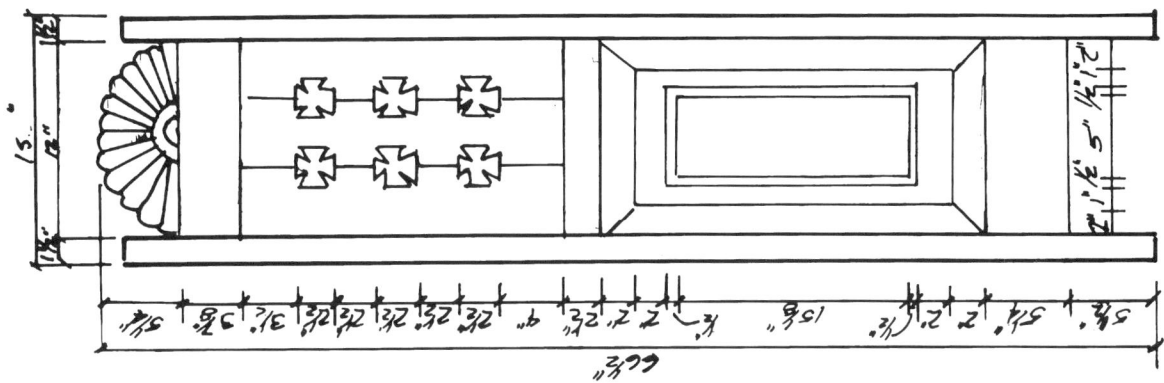

SIDE

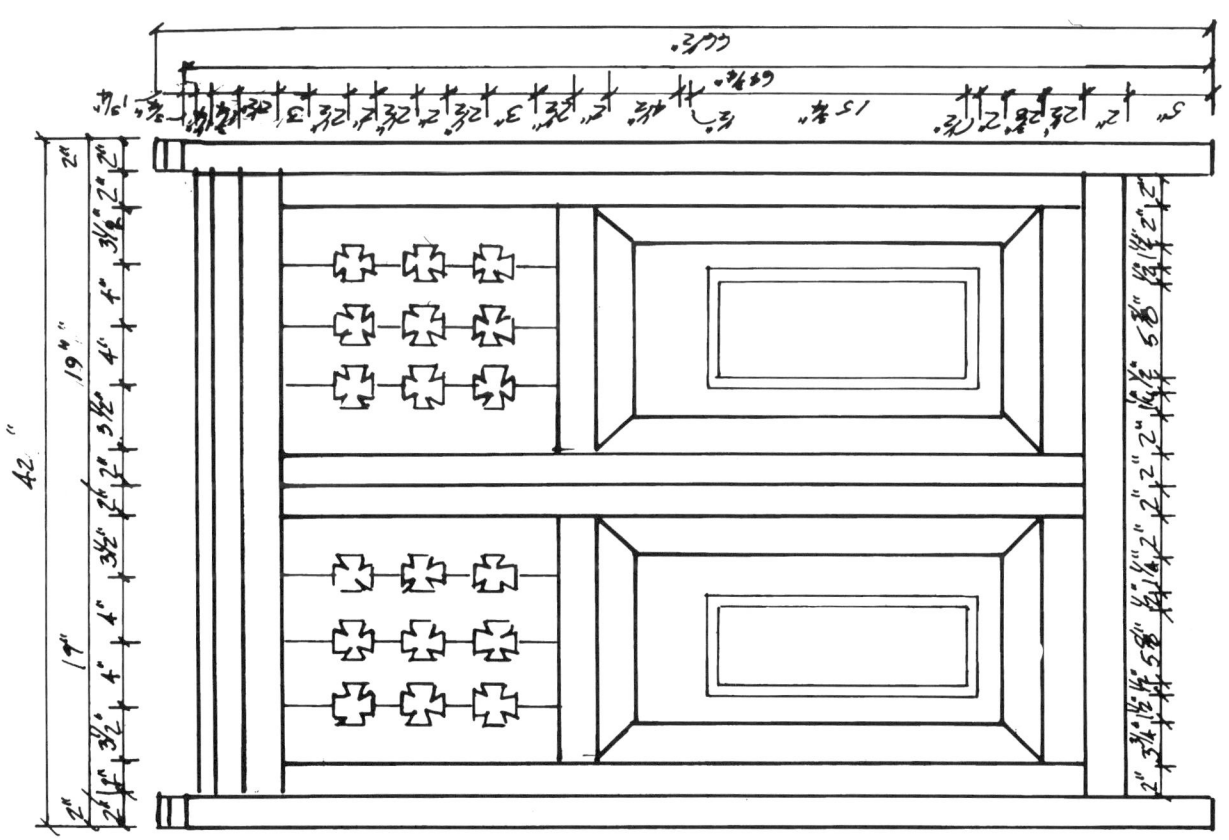

FRONT

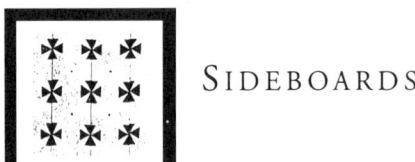

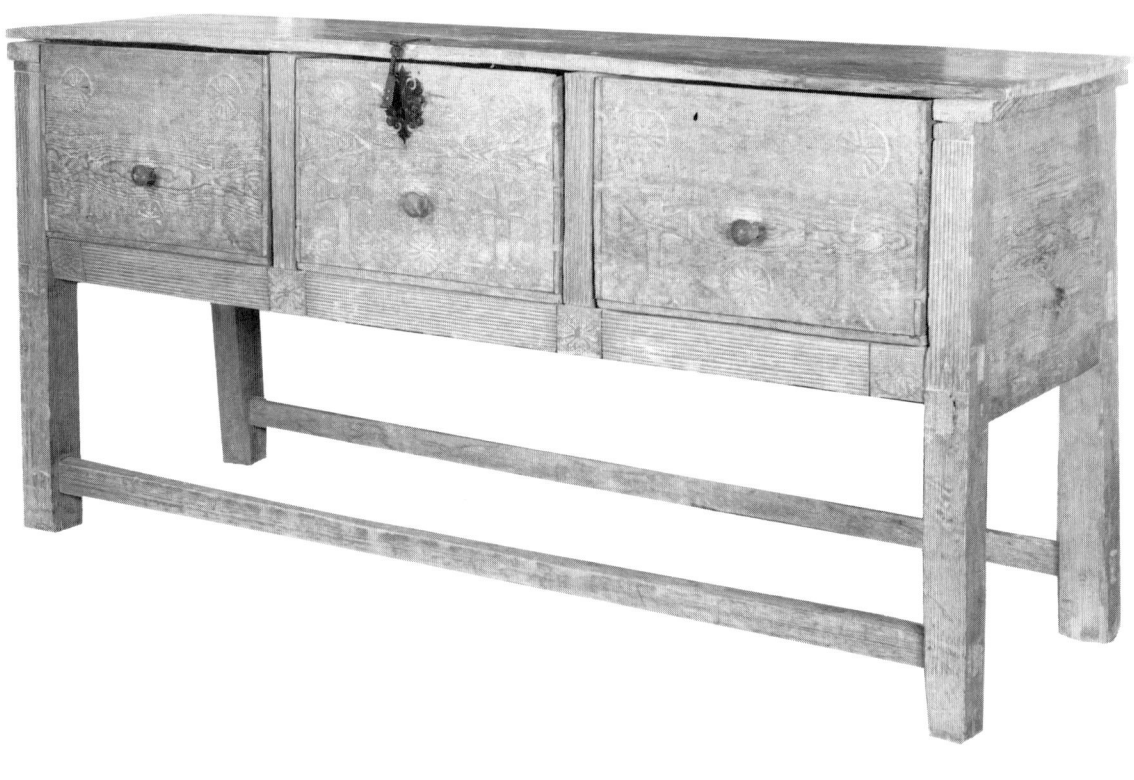

Carved Crosses Sideboard

OFFICIALLY LISTED AS an "irregular wooden table," this is actually a sideboard chest which has three deep drawers with a lock and key securing the middle one. It originally came from the Santa Cruz Church and is estimated to have been built around 1816. Two rosettes carved across the top of each drawer and one below each knob are flanked by two crosses on either side of each knob. A great deal of beading decorates the bottom drawer rail and rosettes are carved into the blocks that separate the drawers. The top sits on a horizontal bar which rests on top of the legs. The top half of the legs have the same beading as seen on the drawer rail. Open mortise-and-tenon joints hold the rails to the legs. The side panel is not framed but is let right into the legs. The drawers are dovetailed boxes. *International Folk Art Foundation Collections at the Museum of International Folk Art, Santa Fe, New Mexico (FW-129).*

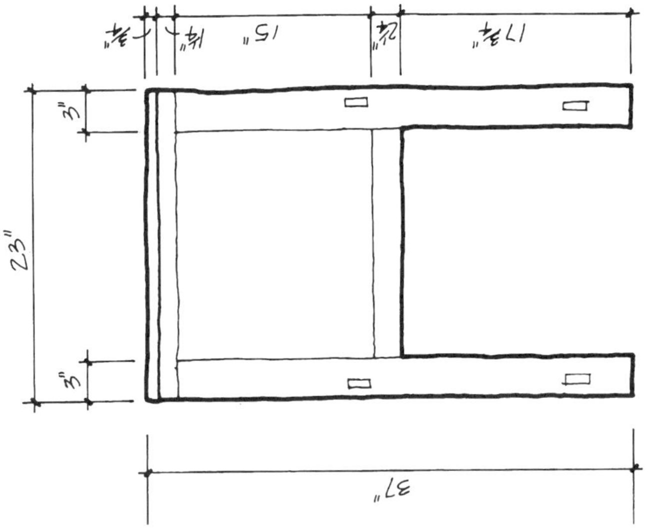

SIDE

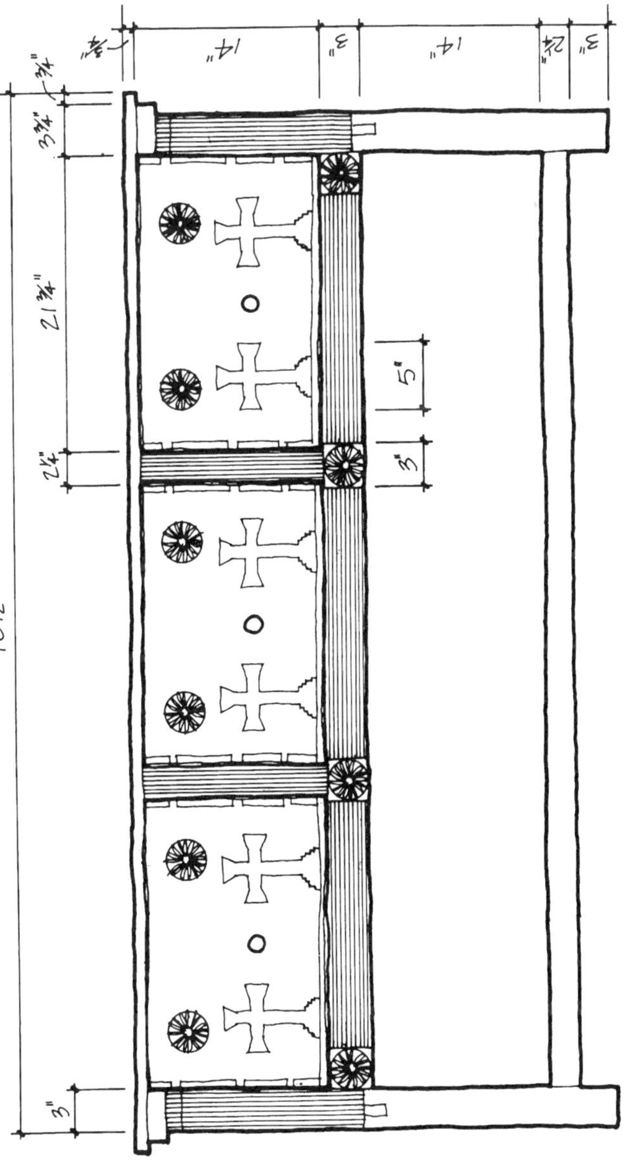

FRONT

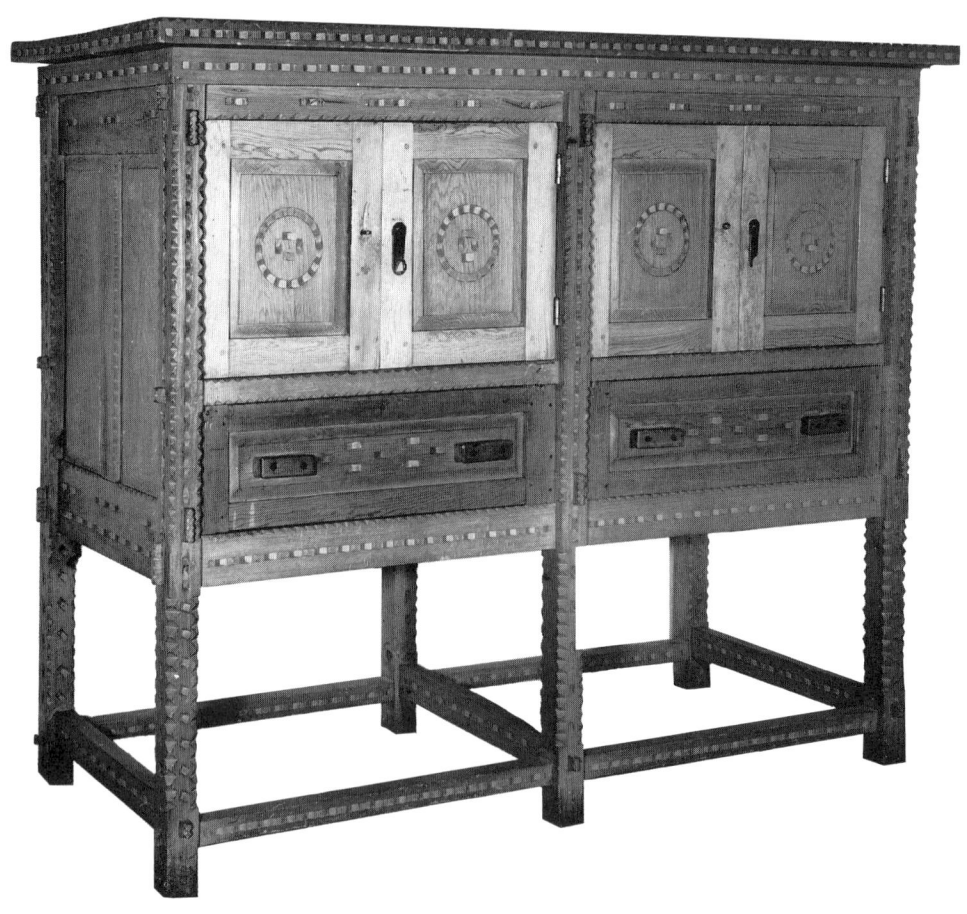

Chip Carved Pueblo Revival/Mission Sideboard

BUILT ORIGINALLY FOR the Women's Board Room of the Museum of Fine Arts in Santa Fe, this enormous sideboard shows all the detailing of the chest (see p. 48) and chair (see p. 74) which were built at the same time. The drawers are just simple boxes decorated false-frame style to give them a raised panel look. *Museum of New Mexico Collections, Museum of International Folk Art, Santa Fe, New Mexico (FW-130).*

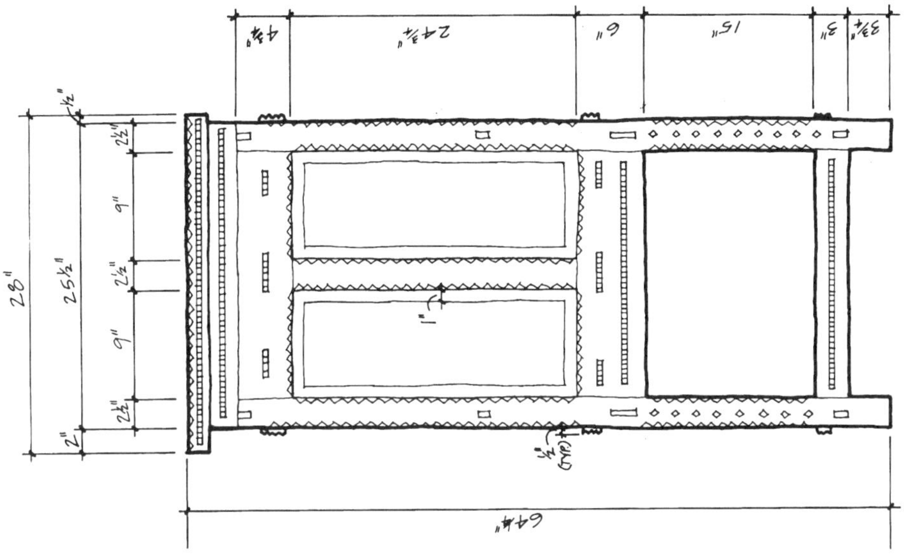

SIDE

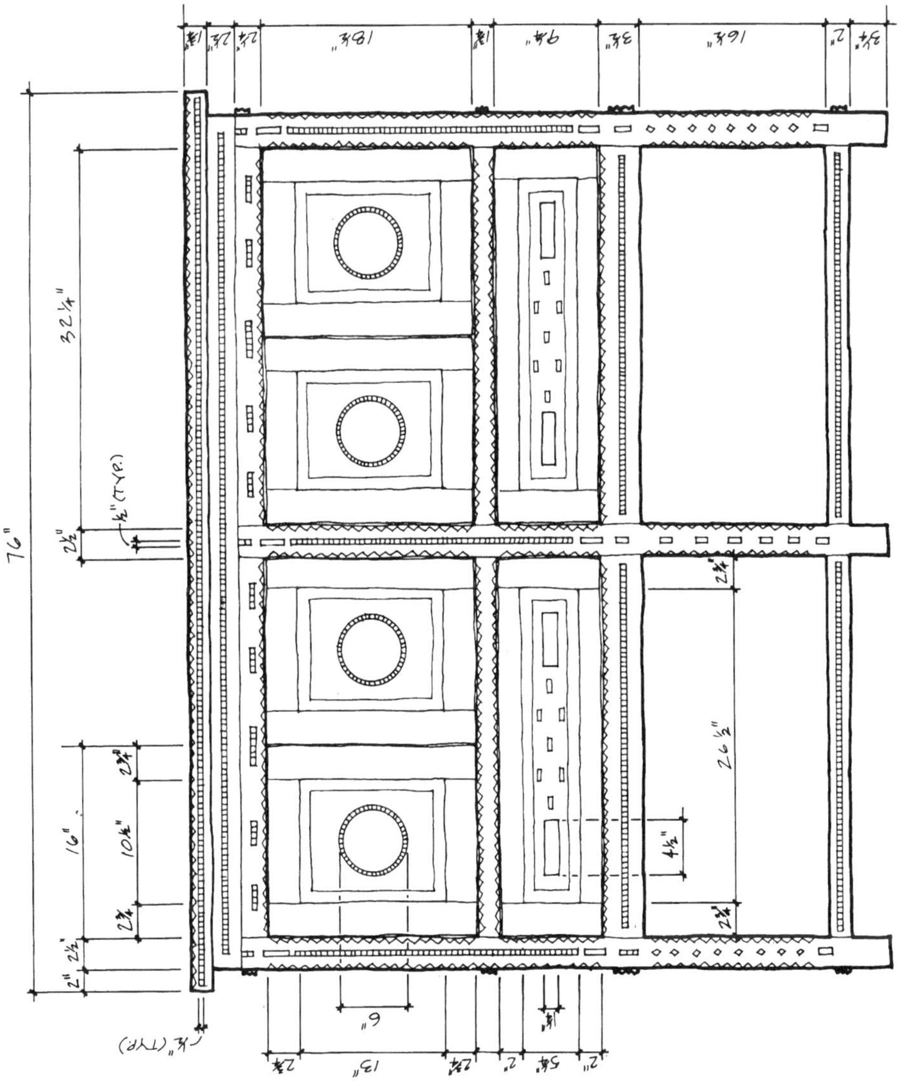

FRONT

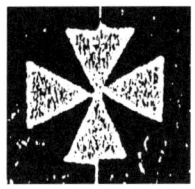

Resources

It can be difficult to show much detail on a 7-foot-long piece of furniture when the drawing must be reduced to a 7-inch page in a book. If you would like to see any given piece in larger scale, a large format, 18-inch by 24-inch blueprint is available for each drawing in this book. Simply fill out a copy of the form below with the code number of the particular piece (available at the end of each text block) and send it with your check for $6.00 per drawing to Fine Additions, Inc., 2405 Maclovia Lane, Santa Fe, New Mexico 87505. If you have any further questions, feel free to phone the author at (505) 471-4549.

FW NO.	NAME OF PIECE	PAGE	PRICE

Please add $3.50 Shipping and Handling per order $3.50

TOTAL

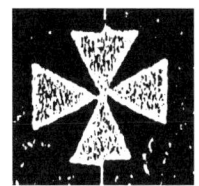

Bibliography

BUNTING, BAINBRIDGE. *Early Architecture in New Mexico.* Albuquerque: University of New Mexico Press, 1976.

HAMMETT, KINGSLEY. *Crafting New Mexican Furniture.* Santa Fe: Red Crane Books, 1994.

KATZ, SALI. *Furniture from the Hispanic Southwest.* Santa Fe: Ancient City Press, 1984.

MATHER, CHRISTINE, AND SHARON WOODS. *Santa Fe Style.* New York: Rizzoli, 1986.

NESTOR, SARAH. *The Native Market of the Spanish Colonial Furniture Bulletin.* Santa Fe: The Colonial New Mexico Historical Foundation, 1978.

NEW MEXICO STATE BOARD FOR VOCATIONAL EDUCATION. *Spanish Colonial Furniture Bulletin.* Santa Fe: State Board for Vocational Education, 1933.

TAYLOR, LONN, AND DESSA BOKIDES. *Carpinteros and Cabinetmakers: Furniture Making in New Mexico, 1600-1900.* Santa Fe: Museum of International Folk Art, 1984.

TAYLOR, LONN, AND DESSA BOKIDES. *New Mexican Furniture, 1600-1940: The Origins, Survival, and Revival of Furniture Making in the Hispanic Southwest.* Santa Fe: Museum of New Mexico Press, 1987.

VEDDER, ALAN C. *Furniture of Spanish New Mexico.* Santa Fe: Sunstone Press, 1977.

WARREN, NANCY HUNTER. *New Mexico Style: A Source Book of Traditional Architectural Details.* Santa Fe: Museum of New Mexico Press, 1986.

WILLIAMS. A.D. *Spanish Colonial Furniture.* Salt Lake City: Gibbs M. Smith, Inc., 1982.

WROTH, WILLIAM, ED. *Furniture From The Hispanic Southwest.* Santa Fe: Ancient City Press, 1984.

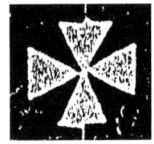

Index

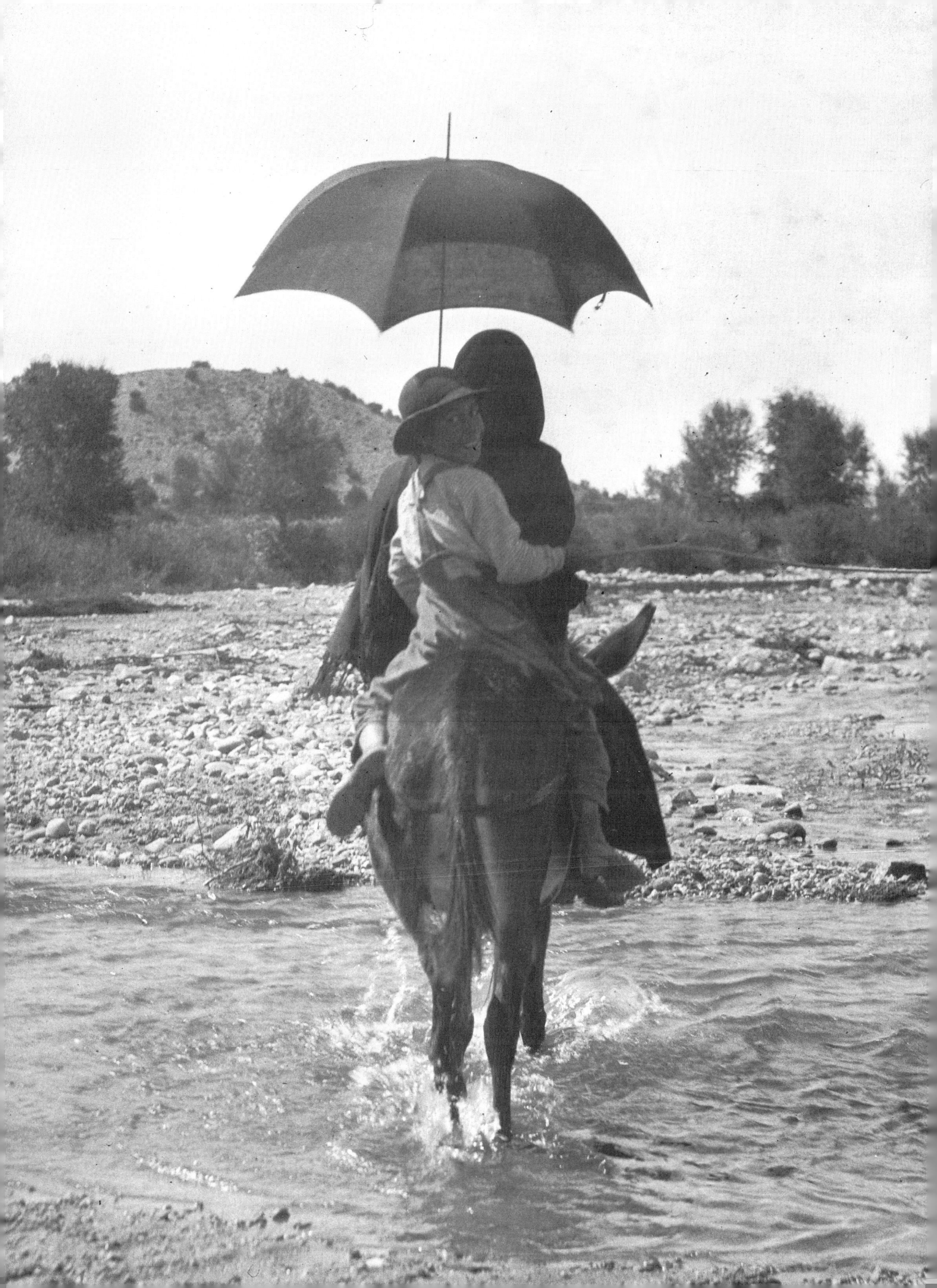

Crafting
NEW MEXICAN
FURNITURE

A GUIDE TO BUILDING FURNITURE IN THE SOUTHWEST STYLE
BY KINGSLEY HAMMETT

Kingsley Hammett's handsome new book [Crafting New Mexican Furniture] teaches us the fundamentals of New Mexican design while presenting us with more than two dozen projects, many of which feature beautiful carved sunbursts and rosettes. You're sure to find a project that, when completed, will add cheer to some room in your home.

Hugh Foster, Contributing Editor
Popular Woodworking, January 1996

Thank you for writing such a wonderful book! I've been searching for a hobby and decided to make my own southwestern furniture but was unable to find any information on the subject. I finally came across your book at the public library and liked it so much that I went out and purchased it.

Susan Mazzotti
Glendale, Arizona

26 PROJECTS ALONG WITH COMPLETE INFORMATION
ON TOOLS, MATERIALS, DESIGN DETAILS, EMBELLISHMENTS, AND JOINTS.

SEND $19.95 PLUS $3.50 S/H TO:

FLEETWOOD PRESS
2405 MACLOVIA LANE
SANTA FE, NEW MEXICO 87505
505.471.4549